FORUM FAVORITES

• • • • • • • • • • •

VOLUME 4

Al-Anon Family Group Headquarters, Inc.

New York • 1993

The Al-Anon Family Groups are a fellowship of relatives and friends of alcoholics who share their experience, strength and hope in order to solve their common problems. We believe alcoholism is a family illness and that changed attitudes can aid recovery.

Al-Anon is not allied with any sect, denomination, political entity, organization or institution; does not engage in any controversy, neither endorses nor opposes any cause. There are no dues for membership. Al-Anon is self-supporting through its own voluntary contributions.

Al-Anon has but one purpose: to help families of alcoholics. We do this by practicing the Twelve Steps, by welcoming and giving comfort to families of alcoholics, and by giving understanding and encouragement to the alcoholic.

The Suggested Preamble to the Twelve Steps

For information and catalog of literature write:

AL-ANON FAMILY GROUP HEADQUARTERS, INC.
P.O. BOX 862, MIDTOWN STATION
NEW YORK, NEW YORK 10018-0862
212-302-7240
FAX 212-869-3757

Library of Congress Catalog Card No. 91-72776
ISBN-910034-90-7
© AL-ANON FAMILY GROUP HEADQUARTERS, INC. 1993

 Approved by
World Service Conference
Al-Anon Family Groups

1-30M-93-5.00   **B–9d**   Printed in U.S.A.

Contents

• • • • • • • • • •

Introduction

*T*his fourth volume of FORUM FAVORITES is a true "grass roots effort." In December 1991, The FORUM asked readers to submit titles of their favorite FORUM articles (1954-1990). The response was so overwhelming that we had to shorten the time frame to 1954 through 1979!

FORUM FAVORITES, Volume 4 is the final result. It represents members' all-time favorites—the best of the best. In this, you will find such legendary sharings as "The Elephant in the Living Room" and "The Prince Frog." You will also find articles on the Slogans, the Steps, and the Traditions—and a special collection of "Cogent Comments."

All these are, of course, intended to deepen our understandings of Al-Anon principles. But they are also intended to provide a kind of kinship—a personal connection to each author and a sense of identification with the experiences each author shares. We hope you will find the articles that are featured here as timeless now as they were when they first appeared.

• • • • • • • • • •

Working The Program

*I*t's funny. Now that I've been working my
program for two years, I look at my husband and see
a loving, productive, caring person. Has he changed
all that much, or is it my attitude that has made
all the difference?

ACCEPTANCE

The Elephant in the Living Room

So there the dumb thing sits—it's called alcoholism, and it's the biggest thing in the house. Other people can entertain, other children can have friends sleep over. Your house is full of elephant!

So you flail at it, cry over it, push the tail end, pull the trunk end, and try to coax it into joining the circus—but there the dumb thing sits.

Some of us spend so much time pushing and pulling our own private pachyderm around that we never really do anything else. Our children go on with their lives the best they can, and every now and then we leave off shoving long enough to throw a little comment or criticism at them—but we run back to our primary occupation.

Now, isn't that silly? You can't move an elephant! You can move out—or you can go on with your life the best way possible considering the irrefutable fact that there is an elephant in your living room. You can learn to live with it—roller skate around it—dust it off—crochet a nose-cosy for it—paint it puce and purple—rent space on it to the political candidate of your choice—but STOP TRYING TO MOVE IT!!!—and smile. God loves you, and He gave you the whole world to be happy in, not just the little space around the you-know-what in your you-know-where.

● ● ● ● ● ● ● ● ● ●

Some Thoughts On Acceptance

Acceptance does not necessarily mean approval. It is not grim endurance, clenched-teeth resignation. Acceptance is a calm appraisal of reality: this is the way it is; now what shall I do about it?

Accepting reality means finding out what my choices are. Best not to choose something that isn't one of my available options at the time! Once I accept a situation or a person, my Higher Power works one of two miracles: He either changes the situation or the person, or He gives me the grace to live with it as it is. Either miracle will do.

Real acceptance enables me to thank my Higher Power for the problem, knowing that He will bring good out of it for all concerned.

ATTITUDES

Grow Where You Are Planted

Tonight our meeting was on letting go. The discussion concerned what to do with a marriage affected by active alcoholism. It returned me to those first three or four years in the program where I kept avoiding that type of discussion.

I had lived through the divorce of my parents and was terribly afraid of the unhappiness of being physically alone, although I don't know any time I was more lonesome than in the days of living with an actively drinking partner.

There was a sign on the table of my first Al-Anon meeting which, although not a regular slogan, has been of help to me— "Grow Where You Are Planted." It was illustrated with a flower.

● ● ● ● ● ● ● ● ● ●

That saying helped me learn it was not my mental or environmental conditions that needed changing. It was me, my attitudes toward my circumstances that had to be faced. Whether I moved in or out of my marriage, my job or any other situation, was not nearly as important as learning to handle whatever was before me.

This slogan, like the other slogans, said slow down, stop, think, reevaluate and then start again. I slowly was able to get off my merry-go-round of anxieties and begin working the problems of my life one day at a time.

A Step To Maturity

I almost picked up my dolls and left Al-Anon *for good.* I had dominated the group, monopolized meetings and tried to turn the screws in the heads of other members, but I *talked* good Al-Anon.

When some more experienced members told me I took the alcoholic's inventory more than mine, I felt hurt. I went home and vowed never to return. I forgot how many times I had told others, "To deal with hurt, look to see if you did anything wrong. If you didn't, simply refuse to take offense. But if you did, you must make amends, and the hurt will diminish."

I wanted to punish these people by taking away my little gems of wisdom until I remembered that retaliation boomerangs. I needed the group more than the group needed me.

So I took another step to maturity as I continue to recover from my illness of not listening. I am so quick to perceive what I suffer from others, and so slow to notice what others suffer from me.

• • • • • • • • • •

What Al-Anon Won't Do

Al-Anon will not change your spouse, but it will help you to change yourself and your attitude.

Al-Anon will not work for your spouse, but it will work for you if you keep coming to meetings and keep an open mind.

Al-Anon will not help you unless you remember you are powerless over alcohol and the alcoholic.

Al-Anon cannot be worked in a week, a month or even a year, but working the program one day at a time will help you to realize one day is just about all you can handle at one time. So be prepared for a lifetime with Al-Anon.

Al-Anon will not get you back to church or religion, but it can help you find the God of your understanding and then you can take it from there.

Al-Anon does not control the alcoholic, but you can learn to *Let Go and Let God* take control.

There are seven little words that have a very big meaning for the first three Steps. They are: I can't; He can, so let Him. I can't take credit for these words; I borrowed them from a recovering alcoholic. They have helped me so much. I hope they help you too.

Two Important Factors

Before Al-Anon I was afraid to speak up. All I ever did was shut up and build up my store of resentment, feeding my self-pity and martyrdom. In Al-Anon I learned I don't have to shut up and put up. However, two factors are vital when speaking up: 1. How important is it? So often we lose our perspective and make mountains out of molehills. 2. How and when do I

• • • • • • • • • •

speak out? If I jump on my husband the minute he comes in the door, I will have been instrumental in starting an argument.

I have found the courage to change what I can—me. I slowly overcame the fear of expressing my feelings to my spouse. Now I do it in a matter-of-fact way. Both before sobriety and since, I have been able to *get it off my chest* without worrying about his returning to the bottle. But I try to do it in the right spirit. I honestly don't think that speaking out in the manner I have described is counter to Al-Anon philosophy. Yes, we learn to keep our mouths shut, but not permanently zippered!

No Prince Charming

When my husband stopped drinking and joined AA, I expected him to be loving, responsive, responsible, active, interested, super-human. Instead, I found myself living with someone who slept, watched TV, took walks ten times a day, and turned away from my affectionate hugs.

Al-Anon helped me to stop watching and criticizing him, thinking how lazy he was. Instead, I learned to be grateful for his sobriety and turn the spotlight on myself. I found the courage to begin projects myself, doing things I enjoyed instead of sitting home moping.

Chairing meetings helped me to grow. I've learned to be good to myself. But practicing patience and faith have been hardest for me. When my husband would turn away from my affectionate advances I had to work on my feelings of rejection, resentment and self-pity. I had to accept his disease and his moods, and refrain from retaliation by maintaining a loving attitude. The slogans, prayer, and talking to Al-Anon friends, especially my sponsor, helped a lot.

As a result, I have time and energy to share with others.

• • • • • • • • • •

Instead of waiting impatiently for my husband's mood to change, I give love elsewhere and get help in return. By making myself available to others, sharing my serenity and asking for help when I need it, I have become less nervous, more content, more loving and more open to receive love.

It's funny. Now that I've been working my program for two years, I look at my husband and see a loving, productive, caring person. Has he changed all that much, or is it my attitude that has made the difference?

Don't Misinterpret: This Is A Selfish Program

I recently heard a woman at a meeting say that her life had completely changed since Al-Anon. She seemed happy and was determined to stay that way at any cost, no matter whom she had to step on to keep herself *up.*

She said that after seeing the change in her, her husband asked her if she could help him, and invited her to accompany him to an AA meeting. She replied that she was so proud of what she had done for herself, she wasn't sharing it with anyone, and told him, "After all, it's a selfish program. I have mine, get yours." I thought I was hearing things!

I believe this is the wrong attitude, and the opposite of what the program teaches us. If we want to be able to handle our problems, we must take care of ourselves first. We can't even think straight until we can be still and feel right within ourselves. We must keep our spirits up and maintain our serenity, but also be compassionate and loving towards everyone.

Another way this expression *selfish program* is misinterpreted is when people use it as an excuse to leave small children alone while they go out to a movie, dinner, or even a meeting. Members ought to be sure their obligations are taken care of before they let go and expect God to take care of their

● ● ● ● ● ● ● ● ● ●

children. The slogans are great, but we need to use common sense, too. *Selfish program* means it's for us. We are here for ourselves, to make better people of ourselves, to live better, love better and learn that there can be joy in spite of apparent chaos.

Handling The Blahs

*H*ow do you handle these blah periods when you've changed from an eager, loving, seeking Al-Anon member into a plodding, phlegmatic bench-warmer?

I work on attitude. I accept myself as I am at the moment, without feeling guilty. I remind myself that boredom is self-centeredness; that perhaps the people who were there at my first meeting didn't want to be there either—but they were!

I go to meetings other than my own. I hunt up my sponsor; talk to newcomers. I reread the literature. And then I turn the situation over to my Higher Power.

Courtesy Is Contagious

*M*y sponsor told me to put a little courtesy in my life. While I had managed to maintain a courteous but phony manner toward some people, to those near and dear to me courtesy was forgotten.

It was hard for me at first but I worked at it with my children and then my neighbors. It got to be rather nice, and I felt a whole lot better. I got a good feeling about myself and even began to have fun.

• • • • • • • • • •

But courtesy toward my husband was a different story. I'd become indifferent toward him and my first attempts at courtesy were cold, with malice and contempt. I started slowly, by setting a place for him at the table and keeping his dinner hot. Then I thought of leaving a light on at night before going to bed when he'd still be out.

The night-time lights stopped. I slept more readily and was in a much better frame of mind in the morning. Courtesy to my loved ones made me feel so much better and I found out that it is contagious.

Old-timer Needs Daily Program Too

At one time I got so busy that I decided I didn't really need to read my Al-Anon literature. I even lent my *One Day At A Time In Al-Anon* to another member for several months, telling her I didn't need it at the present time.

Well, things began to go wrong, frustration entered in, there was friction between my husband and me, and everything seemed to be working against me. A dear friend in AA spotted the problem and wisely suggested I get back to the literature. Would you believe I received message after message aimed right at my problems? I received a powerful spiritual message too, and now I don't care how busy I am, or how well things seem to be—I read my literature.

I'm also attending meetings regularly, even though I'm what they call an *old-timer.* We are *old-timers* all right, if we forget we need the program. It is a program for living every day, not just when we think we may need it.

• • • • • • • • • •

DEPRESSION

Overcoming Depression With Some Natural Antidepressants

We asked for articles on coping with depression, since it is such a common problem among Al-Anon members. The response was tremendous. Some members wrote of having been depressed and suicidal since childhood; others, of having become desperate and hopeless before Al-Anon, when they tried unsuccessfully to cope with active alcoholism. Still others wrote of having become despondent after Al-Anon and even after sobriety. It seems depression can strike anyone at any time, and is not necessarily related to the circumstances in which we find ourselves.

The causes of depression also varied widely. Some felt their depression was due to anger or guilt. Others, to self-centeredness, self-pity, resentment, envy or self-hatred. Also cited were boredom, trying to control others, having unreasonably high expectations of ourselves, not living in the present, and discouragement. Some could see a pattern in their depressions: they came in cycles; or coincided with physical changes; or followed periods of elation when the person tended to become complacent and take serenity for granted.

Although there were almost as many ways of coping with depression as there were letters, several respondents said the same thing. A summary of the ideas expressed follows:

Talk It Out
Most said that talking to someone was helpful. They suggested calling an Al-Anon member or seeing a professional. The latter was recommended by several members, especially those whose depressions had dated back to before they met the al-

• • • • • • • • • •

coholic, or to their childhoods, and those whose depressions were particularly persistent or severe, causing them to become suicidal.

Count Blessings

Also high on the list was gratitude. Some recommended making a list of things to be grateful for, and rereading it when feeling down. One person even suggested thanking God for the depression and the insights to be gained from it, remembering that problems are opportunities for growth, and growth hurts. The basic idea was that depression involves negative thinking, and that it's hard to think negative thoughts when we're busy counting our blessings.

Be Good To Self

Many of the suggestions fell in the category of being good to oneself. Among the recommended activities were:

• Treat yourself to something new, preferably something slightly extravagant, something that will make you feel special.

• Make a list of things you like to do and do one.

• Have lunch with a special friend, or plan a get-together with a few people whose company you enjoy.

• Be with happy people.

• Give yourself something to look forward to.

• Develop an interest in something that will give you a sense of satisfaction and enjoyment: a garden, a craft, a hobby.

• Keep yourself looking your best, even if you stay at home all day.

Fitness

Several people stressed physical fitness: getting a check-up to make sure you're not ill; jogging and exercising to get the

• • • • • • • • • •

lead out; getting plenty of rest and avoiding fatigue; skating; swimming; sports in general.

Others concentrated on mental fitness: learning to use your public library; reading self-help books; becoming assertive; forgiving yourself; remembering a good experience or a joy and concentrating on that; making sure that your behavior is in agreement with your values; controlling your thoughts and forcing yourself to avoid negative thinking.

Spiritual fitness was also mentioned by many: taking time each day for meditation; praying and establishing conscious contact with God as we understand Him; reading inspirational literature; praying for compassion.

Get Busy
Apparently, many people find that just getting up and doing something is an answer. Some recommended making a list of everything that had to be done in one day (keeping it within reasonable limits, of course), and then doing one thing at a time and crossing it off the list as you go along. Going for walks, appreciating the beauty of nature, scrubbing floors—all kinds of active and passive things were mentioned. The idea is to get your mind off yourself.

But the most popular exercise of all seemed to be doing something for someone else without expecting anything in return. Specifically mentioned were: doing volunteer work; going out speaking and doing a kind deed each day.

Specifics
Finally, here are some specific suggestions:

• Accept the depression. Don't bother to try to understand it or fight it.

• Hold your shoulders back and chin up; it's harder to be depressed in that position.

• Accept the fact that although you may be ready to let by-

• • • • • • • • • • •

gones be bygones, others may not be.

- Inhale and say, "Breathe in God's goodness." Exhale and say, "Breathe out all trouble and woe."

- Believe that all your days are good; it's just that some are better than others.

- Say "I love you" to the person who is upsetting you.

- Remember, *This Too Shall Pass.* Our Higher Power gives us what we need each day. He wants what's best for us. We are precious to Him.

The Program

All of the above suggestions were submitted in the spirit of *sharing our experience, strength and hope* as we are taught to do in the program. When deciding whether or not to try something that has worked for someone else, it's important to consider where we're coming from. For instance, if we're constantly running, engaged in frantic activity, the suggestion to *get busy* certainly does not apply. And just filling our day with any kind of activity might not be the answer either.

Some of the suggestions offered may seem to have little to do with Al-Anon, and even to be a little gimmicky. We need to remember that, although gimmicks and tricks may help, nothing replaces a serious study and diligent application of the Steps and Slogans. Many letters dealt with this and recommended increasing attendance at meetings, reading the literature and working the program. Here are some ways in which we can apply the program to overcome depression:

Step One. If our depression stems from feelings of frustration, resentment and hopelessness derived from trying to control the alcoholic, acceptance of our powerlessness and placing the focus on ourselves will do much to relieve it.

Step Two. If our depression stems from feelings of self-

• • • • • • • • • • •

pity and the conviction that we are all alone, that no one cares, then a belief in a loving Higher Power who can restore us to sanity is what we need. We can come to believe that we are worthy of love in and of ourselves. We can develop a positive faith.

Step Three. If our depression stems from the inability to detach from fear of what will happen if we're not in control, then turning our wills and our lives over to the care of God will enable us to let go and find the inner peace that faith brings.

Step Four. If our depression is the result of blaming others for our unhappiness, then taking a fearless moral inventory will place the responsibility squarely where it belongs—on our own shoulders.

Step Five. If our depression comes from the fear that we are unlovable and unacceptable, then opening ourselves up to another will mark the beginning of allowing others to love us so we can love ourselves. It encourages us to talk instead of hurt.

Steps Six and Seven. If our depression comes from an overgrown sense of responsibility, allowing our Higher Power to help us overcome our defects will place our responsibility in its proper perspective.

Step Eight. If our depression derives from negative thinking, self-pity and the conviction that we have been taken advantage of, then making a list of those we have harmed and becoming willing to make amends to them, turns our minds to those things over which we do have control.

Step Nine. If our depression stems from guilt feelings, making amends will go a long way toward evening the score.

Step Ten. If our depression is recurring, then constant vigilance is what we need.

• • • • • • • • • •

Step Eleven. For an emptiness of spirit, a lack of faith or purpose, the answer is in establishing conscious contact with God, praying only for the knowledge of His will and the power to carry that out.

Step Twelve. For those who wish to lead meaningful lives, who need to be busy, carrying the message, in all its various ways, certainly offers limitless opportunities.

Easy Does It is good for those of us who expect too much from ourselves and whose depressions derive from feelings of failure and frustration.

Let Go and Let God is made to order for those of us whose depressions are the result of trying to control everyone and everything.

One Day at a Time corrects the problems stemming from guilt over the past or fear of the future.

But for the Grace of God reminds us to count our blessings, and to maintain a grateful attitude.

Let It Begin with Me reaffirms that we are responsible for our own happiness; that it's up to us to start the ball of recovery rolling by getting well ourselves.

DETACHMENT

Loving Detachment

I discovered I couldn't detach with love until I got rid of the anger I'd accumulated towards my husband. Then I understood that the love referred to in the phrase *detach with love* is not romantic love, but a more stable, steady love which allows us to care for and help others although we don't like their behavior.

● ● ● ● ● ● ● ● ● ●

To me, this means I must provide secure surroundings for the alcoholic while he wrestles with his problems; I must show him by my behavior that I love him; I must know where help is available when he asks for it. To someone else, it might mean breaking off the relationship. We all must base our decisions on our own situations.

Detachment From Children: What It Is And Isn't

*D*etachment is a positive attitude I must consistently work on in my relationships with other people. It is not a last resort in my effort to maintain serenity.

Where my children are concerned, detachment is not emotional abandonment nor lack of guidance. It is my release of them from constant demands that they conform to my idea of how they should think, feel and act. I must allow them freedom to be individuals, freedom to be wrong at times.

I thought I had to save everyone from hurt and direct all family activity. Now I try really to listen to my children without absorbing their hurt or telling them how to straighten everything out. I allow them to grow by making decisions suitable for their own age. Often their decisions are good and they have the satisfaction of knowing they are capable and responsible.

I hope they sense that whatever the outcome of their decisions, they are loved. Two precious gifts we give our children are roots and wings.

• • • • • • • • • •

Swamps And Other Dark Watery Places

Once upon a time there was a happy young couple with three lovely children. They lived on a grassy hillside beside a large dark swamp. Day by day the father, through no fault of his own, found himself drawn into the swamp. Finally he was ac-

tually living each day in that dark dreary mire. In an effort to help, and knowing no better, the wife followed him into the swamp. Here they lived amidst the mire and weeds. She spent many hours preaching to him, telling him how muddy he looked, how lazy he was, how she hated living in a swamp and how unfair this all was. She even threatened to leave him but, of course, never did.

Her appearance slowly grew worse and worse. Her hair became wet and stringy; her clothes hung limp; her sad face was caked with mud. She changed from a happy, loving, caring person to a self-pitying grouch, full of hatred and resentment. Occasionally she would look up from the swamp with sad, tired eyes and see their children sitting on the hillside. She was too busy worrying to pay much attention to them. Once in a while she did notice they were moving nearer and nearer the swamp themselves.

Then one day an Al-Anon member came and told her she did not have to live in the swamp, that she had a right to live where she chose. So gradually she left the swamp. She washed the mud from her hair and face, changed her wet clothes and began to take a real interest in herself and the world around her. She played with the children on the hillside and they all

● ● ● ● ● ● ● ● ● ●

planted flowers so it looked even prettier. The children were so pleased to have their mother back they began playing and laughing like normal kids. They all felt badly that dad was still living in the swamp because they loved him very much and showed him their love every chance they got.

Maybe someday he will see the green hillside, the pretty flowers and his happy family, and he will join them. Until that day and for all days thereafter, mother will continue to keep in touch with her Al-Anon friends so that she can enjoy each day as a God-given miracle, never to be wasted in a swamp.

Detachment—What Does It Mean To You?

Often heard in Al-Anon is the word detachment. Twenty-one pages are devoted to it in *One Day At A Time In Al-Anon.* Yet, it continues to be misunderstood and misinterpreted.

We have all been emotionally involved with alcoholics—dependent on them for our happiness, and then crippled by the need to control them. It's no wonder detachment is difficult to understand and even harder to achieve. It sometimes becomes the excuse for emotional withdrawal, bitter revenge, icy lack of interest.

But detachment really is love at its most productive, most free and best. It is caring enough about others to allow them to be themselves and to learn through their mistakes. It is being responsible for one's own feelings and welfare. It is being able to make decisions without the ulterior motive of influencing others or fearing their reaction.

True detachment is based on faith in a Higher Power who will work things out for the best if we but do our best. There is no need, then, for worry; for guilt when things don't turn out as planned; no need for fear.

• • • • • • • • • • •

Concerned by the frequent misinterpretation of the word detachment in Al-Anon, some members prefer to say release with love. Those words convey more warmth—caring without possessing, concern without domination, involvement without suffocation.

Allowing alcoholics to face the painful consequences of their drinking or, in sobriety, of unacceptable behavior, in the knowledge that this pain is necessary for their recovery, and doing it without rancor or sentimentality—this is release with love.

An Alateen Speaks On Detachment

Detachment means to get away from the other person's problem, not away from the person. It is adjusting to things as they are, and loving without interfering. It is forgetting about past regrets and resentments, and not worrying about the future.

Some people think if you have resentments and are angry toward the other person, it is easier to detach. But that isn't so. If you're still angry and resentful, you're not detached at all.

Detachment can help alcoholics to reach the point where they ask for help. As long as they have someone to run their lives for them, they don't have to.

Detachment helps me to listen instead of react to what people say. I can listen to helpful advice and screen out the things I don't like. When I'm challenged to an argument, I detach and leave the other person standing there wondering why I didn't take him up on the challenge. That's as good as winning the argument.

Detachment has brought me peace of mind. Now that I'm not trying to run everyone else's life, I have more time for my-

● ● ● ● ● ● ● ● ● ●

self. And most of all, detachment has helped me to love without trying to possess. In short, detachment can be defined as *mind your own business.*

Disappointment Leads To Detachment

*L*eaving my husband, who has been sober in AA for 18 months, at home, I attended a weekend Al-Anon Roundup with Al-Anon friends. After the weekend, I felt so wonderful that, at first, I didn't want to share my good feelings with anyone—I wanted to keep them all to myself.

Just the same, I was disappointed when there was no one waiting eagerly at the door to welcome me back when I returned home. I put the car away, unloaded my luggage, struggled to unlock the doors, and as I entered, heard a loud snoring noise from the den. Instead of thinking of my husband with resentment, it occurred to me that this was the man who was responsible for all the good things that had happened to me.

After I found a box of candy and lovely card from him on my dresser, I was filled with a need to share my wonderful feelings about the weekend with him. But when I tried, he turned me off. He'd had a bad time while I was away and just wasn't interested. He obviously resented having been left alone.

Later that evening he vented his anger at me in front of AA friends who had dropped in, and threatened to take me to court if I got more involved in Al-Anon. I was completely deflated and angry as his angry outburst continued after our friends left. Taking him seriously, I began to feel guilty. I prayed for help to see where I'd been wrong.

The following morning I felt dejected, disgusted with myself, guilty, empty. But I decided to meditate as I do every morning. I read the ODAT page on serenity and counted my

• • • • • • • • • •

blessings. My Higher Power heard my prayer. I had a great sense of peace and conviction that I'd done nothing wrong; my guilty feelings weren't justified. I began to see that my husband is still sick. I must do what is good for me, and that includes giving to Al-Anon what the program has given me.

It is now two months later. My husband is active in AA and much happier. Most important, though, my happiness no longer depends on him. I have finally let go and let God.

DIVORCE

Divorced After Sobriety

I was in Al-Anon six years and my husband was sober when we divorced. It took a lot of thought to come to that decision but we are both happier for it now. Once sobriety enters the home, both parties have a lot of work to do together. Some marriages are impossible to save. Thank God for my Al-Anon friends who helped me through that difficult time. I was criticized and shunned by some who saw me as a threat. Because I wasn't very strong I left Al-Anon, but eventually returned and have stayed ever since.

Although I am now married to a non-alcoholic, I continue to attend meetings because I still have to live with me. Thank you for helping me to feel once again a part of Al-Anon.

On Ending A Marriage—Some Vital Steps

*I*t is never easy to end a relationship, especially such an intimate one as a marriage. So much emotion, effort and caring have been invested. It takes humility and courage to say *it can't work.*

My husband and I were divorced after five years of abstin-

• • • • • • • • • •

ence. Before I could finally decide to leave him, I had to answer some questions to myself.

- Have I done everything I can to make this marriage work?

- Have I really applied the program, being tolerant, communicating honestly, letting go?

- Do I love and desire him as a husband? What do I want from marriage? Is that realistic?

- Am I ready to face the challenge of living alone?

- Can I accept the consequences of this decision, whatever they might be—his support, suicide, or drinking again, non-support or violence? Is growth still possible in this relationship?

- Would the problems of being single be worse than the problems I have now?

- Can I stay in this relationship and maintain my dignity and self-respect?

- If I stay because I am afraid, what will that do to my feelings of self-worth?

There was a lot of guilt to resolve: guilt about walking out on a sober, but sick man; guilt about not being willing to settle for less than what I wanted and felt I deserved; guilt about hurting a man who'd done his best. But I realized that to stay with him out of pity or guilt would strip him of all dignity and would poison our relationship further with anger. Because I loved him as a person, I decided to do what was best for both of us, and trusted my Higher Power to take care of the results.

My Al-Anon friends were wonderful; I couldn't have kept my sanity without the program. The months between the time when I made my decision and the time when my husband actually moved out proved to be even worse than when he was

• • • • • • • • • •

actively drinking. I found that the best way to deal with him was to be pleasant and friendly when he was; to ignore him and leave the room when he became verbally abusive; and to tell him when his behavior made me angry. I went through a period of tremendous anger. Then I went through a period of grief and mourning, during which I felt sad for a long time. I cried as though someone had died. Someone had, of course—the old me and the marriage.

As difficult as it was to follow through on my decision, I am happy I did. I am not lonely—my days are more than full and my life is rich with the love of friends. The children are adjusting amazingly well. I have learned to open myself up, to let people help me, to dare to experience the myriad facets of life which were not available to me before.

Change Is Hard But Worth The Effort

Although my marriage is over, I find my dreams and hopes have not died. Separation, divorce, my husband's engagement—each event put me into my private hell. Even though I believe each of these decisions to be right, they were heart-rending because, to me, they represented failure. But now I believe that holding on to my marriage would have been the real failure.

My children have changed so much in the past six years since we've separated. They've grown from scared insecure beings into mature confident people sure of their right to be themselves. My husband, freed from having to justify his actions to me and given back the burden of the consequences of his actions, chose sobriety in AA.

Although he would have liked a reconciliation, I realized our marriage had failed, not because of his drinking, but because we had separate interests and different priorities. I could

• • • • • • • • • •

not in good conscience go back on what I believe, nor could I ask him to.

When I heard of his plans to remarry, I felt strangely bitter. Why should he be the lucky one—why not me? I began to blame myself and feel sorry for myself. Thank God for Al-Anon. I began to practice *Let Go and Let God*, and *act as if.* I counted my blessings one day at a time. I became truthful to myself. Instead of pushing away my desires as unworthy, I brought them to my Higher Power. I asked Him to help me find a man.

Slowly I realized that, although I still have moments of loneliness, they probably don't occur more often than they did before the marriage broke up. Another person is not the ingredient required for a feeling of completeness. That can only come from within.

I'm not afraid of living alone any more. I've accepted God's will, whatever it is. When I put on makeup and comb my hair, it's because I feel good, not because I want to look good. When I laugh, it's with joy—not to make me *belong.* Suddenly, I see how shallow my life was. This may seem contradictory, but even if I remain alone, it doesn't matter now.

GRATITUDE

Deterrents To Growth

*F*or me the road to growth in Al-Anon has been full of ruts and detours. The first of these was that I came looking for ways to change the alcoholic. Instead of a magic formula, however, I received encouragement, love, and a self-help program.

Then I was discouraged by what I found when I looked at myself. Sometimes I left meetings feeling worse than when I'd come. I resented having to think about all those faults of

• • • • • • • • • •

mine I'd kept hidden or justified for so long. But Al-Anon helped me develop a prodding conscience that wouldn't let me slide back because I was discouraged, tired, or thought I didn't care anymore.

I also ran into trouble when I compared myself to others. I felt discouraged by my slow progress until I realized that, while we all have similar problems, we are all affected differently because we are individuals and we started in different places. I can be grateful for my growth even if it isn't as dramatic or spectacular as someone else's.

If I never progress further (as humble as the progress is that I've made thus far) I'm a far better person today than I was before Al-Anon.

Has Learned A Lot

When I compare my life before and after Al-Anon, it's no surprise which is the winner. I never dreamed the Steps and Slogans could change my life so much, but it's true that we only get out of the program what we put into it. When I just read, went to meetings but didn't keep in touch with members, it didn't work. I had to get involved.

Al-Anon has taught me to enjoy life. When I'm miserable it's usually because I'm forgetting to keep my *hands off* and am reacting to situations over which I have no control.

The program has taught me to be unselfish, to take time out for others and their problems, to pray for them, phone them, and let them know I care. It has taught me to enjoy my children. Before, they were like ornaments on a shelf. I just took time to clean them off. Now I feel good because I can share my love. I have learned to face my faults instead of justifying or hiding behind them. I can laugh at things I didn't think were funny before.

● ● ● ● ● ● ● ● ● ●

The program has brought me closer to God and restored my faith. Before, I thought I was all-powerful, pulling the strings and treating people like puppets. Now I feel stronger because I have a Power greater than myself, who is always there to help out if I let Him.

I can accept responsibility more readily and can also accept my situation without asking *why me.* My demanding has been replaced with gratitude. Instead of being full of fear and going along with things holding resentment in my heart, I can be an individual. I am so grateful to Al-Anon for giving me the chance to have a more manageable, serene life and peace of mind.

Why Keep Coming

*I'*m happily married to a non-alcoholic, am busy with graduate studies, and my mother, now sober a year, lives 2500 miles away. Why do I continue to attend meetings? Gratitude.

Both my mother's sobriety and my present happiness are due in large part to Al-Anon. How can I stop now? Self awareness and spiritual growth are going to continue for the rest of my life. So many people helped me when I first came. How can I not do the same for others?

Cure For Stinking Thinking

*E*ven after a year in Al-Anon, the serenity I searched for continued to elude me. Periodically my thoughts would run wild and, as if someone had pulled a trigger, I would revert to the same old miserable patterns.

Then one day, a long-timer who'd been patiently listening to my stinking thinking said, "You know, if every day you would show gratitude and true gladness for the good in your life,

• • • • • • • • • •

these thoughts wouldn't take over so easily." How simple! Yet how effective.

Never Underestimate the Power of a Woman

Al-Anon has been a vital part of my life for many years, but I am frequently asked why I still go to meetings, since there has been no active problem for sixteen years.

One very good reason is gratitude for those sixteen years of happy sobriety and mutual growth in the programs of AA and Al-Anon.

My second reason is a feeling of responsibility to the new members. Group stability is important: understanding the disease of alcoholism, interpretation of the Twelve Steps and the real meaning of the Traditions are the foundations of Al-Anon. I've been privileged I've had Al-Anon, so I feel I must be there to share that experience.

My third reason is definitely selfish. Al-Anon taught me, many years ago, that I must continue to grow if I wish to live Al-Anon. I don't dare stand still and stagnate, so I use Al-Anon as my bank account. All I have learned is deposited in my mental account. This has grown by small deposits of a serene 24 hours; an acceptance of something I could not change; the use of a God-given idea that has helped someone; a telephone chat that made the day easier for me or for a troubled group member, progress

• • • • • • • • • •

in debunking myself, or new knowledge gained by studying and applying one of the Steps. The interest on this account is mine to use whenever and however I need it. With this I can face disappointments and difficult days, dispel new fears and anxieties and keep my hard-earned serenity.

However, the account itself is to be spent. It is not mine; it was given to me, so I must pass it on to others. Therefore, I have a responsibility to keep making deposits. I know of only one way to do this: living the Al-Anon way of life with the help of others; going to meetings where I see new people searching for what someone there has to give; watching these same people grow out of fear, anxiety and frustration to serenity, faith and positive action, building up their own bank accounts.

HOPE

Second Try Worked

*T*hose of you whose children have tried Alateen only to drop out a few months later need not lose hope. It may be only a temporary situation, as described in the following:

The first time I tried Alateen, I went to meetings to get away from home. After three months, I quit because I felt I wasn't getting anything out of it. After a year and a half, I was self-centered and tense. I was losing most of my friends. When someone explained what Alateen was all about, I decided to give it another try.

I have been a member for three years now and have never been happier. I have come out of my shell, have spoken at open meetings, have learned that alcoholism is a family disease which has affected me, and have learned more about myself. I've even been able to make more friends than ever before. I am so grateful.

● ● ● ● ● ● ● ● ● ●

Expectation vs. Hope

Sometimes a principle of this program is given to me that I can't use right then, either because I haven't grown that much or I don't understand it. One of these was the idea of not expecting anything in order not to be disappointed. I don't want to live never looking forward to anything; I would rather risk disappointment. Only this past year have I come to realize the difference between expectation and hope: expectation says that I am wanting a particular response or reaction from someone, or that I am wanting to write the script for a particular situation; hope says I am eagerly, joyfully anticipating God's handling of my life.

So when I was told not to expect anything, I wasn't being deprived of hope. If I hope and it doesn't happen, I am not devastated because I know that God has other plans, that He is still in charge, and that He wants my good even more than I do. If I burden others with my expectations, on the other hand, I am not admitting my powerlessness, and when things don't go my way, I am, inevitably, disappointed.

LETTING GO

Boomerang

I was having trouble letting go of deep feelings of rejection. The more I tried to get rid of them, the more I had them. Hate, guilt and fear were moving in.

Then I read a story about a boy and his boomerang. When it was old and chipped, his father decided to buy him a new one. The little boy came in crying because he couldn't throw the old boomerang away. Every time he tried, it came back.

• • • • • • • • • •

His father suggested that he just put it down and walk away from it.

I have done the same with my feelings of rejection—and they're gone!

The Prince Frog

Once upon a time, in a nearby land, there lived a fairly fair princess who was young and happy, and full of hope—as most princesses are. She had faults; even people who loved her thought she was a little bossy. But for the most part she was a nice girl—considerate of others, wanting to make something of herself, to enjoy life and to help people.

One magic day she met a prince. It doesn't matter whether people thought he was handsome. To her he was, and he was funny, and smart, and wonderful, and when she was with him, everything was all right with the world, and when she wasn't with him, it wasn't. The prince loved a good time, and drank some. Every now and then the strangest thing would happen. For a fleeting second, she would think he looked like a frog. *How silly*, she thought—if she thought about it at all and so they were married.

The first few years were busy, happy ones. They had children, bought a house, paid off installment loans. They had lots of friends, who had lots of parties, where everybody brought their own bottle, and poker parties, and spaghetti suppers. All their friends drank, and the prince drank a little more than anybody else in the crowd, but everybody said he sure could hold his liquor, and it really didn't seem to interfere with his working or being a good father. When he got a snootful, he would croak at the princess in a rather rude manner. But he was always sorry later and said so. Being croaked at made her nervous, and she developed a couple of warts. She didn't

• • • • • • • • • •

like them, but they weren't very noticeable, and she soon forgot she had them.

As The Prince Turns

It's hard to say exactly when the princess knew that the prince was really turning into a frog. Certainly she knew it long before anybody else. It scared her because she knew nobody would want to be a frog, and she said to herself, *I've got to stop him.*

And she tried. Oh, how she tried. She read up on frogs, and tried to explain to him what was happening, several times a day. She kept track of all the frogs who died of cirrhosis of the liver, and mentioned their names and the cause of their untimely demise at regular intervals. She told him about frogs who lost their jobs, and homes, and businesses, and how sad their families were. She sighed loudly over frogs who committed suicide, and asked him if he didn't think it was a crying shame what drinking could do to a person.

In general, she made his life miserable. She talked about  frogs so much, she seldom talked about anything else, and since that was the one subject he had no intention of talking about, it wasn't long before they didn't have much to say to each other. He felt badly most of the time because liquor had begun to make him feel worse more than it made him feel better, and he croaked more often than he talked. He was so sure she was going to be critical that he tried to criticize first, and she was hurt because she loved him. She got more warts and began to feel ugly and miserable. She never gave up nagging, but she finally decided she couldn't talk him back into being a prince again.

● ● ● ● ● ● ● ● ● ●

War Declared

This is war, she said to herself, and she set out to outwit him, and make him a prince whether he was ready to be one or not. She set herself up as a frog-watcher, and wore herself out trying to keep him from getting liquor. She was so good at bottle-detection, that she could have rented herself out to the revenuers for sniffing out stills. When she found his hidden bottles she poured them out, or made little marks and poured out some and then put water up to the mark. She put Ipecac in a bottle once and waited for him to get deathly sick and swear off forever, but he drank it and never even blinked.

She tried to keep him at home where she could watch him, and when she couldn't, she spent hours calling hospital emergency wards to see if any accident victims had been brought in, and jails to see if anybody had been arrested for drunk driving. She called beer joints and asked the bartender to please get him to the phone because there was an emergency, and then begged him to come home because she thought she heard a burglar on the back porch, or the washing machine was running over, or one of the children had a really bad ingrowing toenail.

Her children were small, and doing cute things, and needing attention. But she was so busy managing the frog full time that she didn't even hear what they said to her lots of times. She worried that they would feel rejected by the frog and begged him not to holler at them. And then when she was upset over his drinking, she would scream at them—*Go away and leave me alone.*

Warts and More Warts

By this time a lot of people were becoming aware that the prince was a frog, and almost everybody could see that the princess had warts. People who didn't know about him thought she was pretty weird. Handling a frog, who keeps hopping and croaking and flinging himself around, makes you go through all kinds of ridiculous motions, and some of the things she

• • • • • • • • • •

did trying to keep him from getting his fool self killed, or jailed, or mutilated made her look like the world's biggest idiot. She knew that and it put her more on the defensive, and her voice rose higher, and she and the frog argued most of the time. The rest of the time they were just living in the same house, enemies, waiting to finish each other off, passing each other and not speaking. They were both sad people, getting older and getting nothing out of life.

The princess was never one to give up, and when she read something in a book about an organization called Al-Anon, she thought to herself, *I wonder if that could help me.* By this time her life was so messed up she had already been to a psychiatrist, was taking tranquilizers, and was so tired of having warts. She knew that because of what had happened to the prince, she had become something she did not want to be. So she found out where Al-Anon met, and she went.

At that first meeting she must have given the older members quite a shock; she was so sure she knew more about frogs than anybody else, and she was ready and willing to help them out by wising them up. She thought none of them was living the way she was, because they looked more or less at peace with themselves. She asked them what else she could possibly do to help the poor prince, and she told them about the warts (as if they hadn't already noticed).

Let Go
"If you want to get rid of the warts," they said, "you've got to let go of the frog." Now, after the first shock, that made sense. Most princesses, after all, are not really stupid, and she had known all the time that the warts were coming from the frog, or at least from the way she was handling the frog. She had thought about letting go, but he had a bad habit of hopping into the road, and bumping into furniture, and she was afraid he would kill himself, and then he'd never get a chance to become a prince again.

● ● ● ● ● ● ● ● ● ●

"But what do I do when he gets drunk?" she asked.

"Nothing," they said.

Well, she thought, *it won't hurt to try.* So the next time she came in and found the frog hopping around and croaking, instead of pointing out the error of his ways, she bit her tongue and smiled and said, "Hi, frog."

"Go to hell," said the frog.

A lot of good that did me, she thought, and promptly squeezed down on the frog again, managing his hopping the best she could, protecting him, and doing what she thought was her duty—and getting warts.

She kept going to Al-Anon though, because she wanted to find out why those other people (who really did have husbands almost as bad as hers) seemed to be in better shape than she was.

Every time she went to a meeting, she'd tell herself that she was better. At first, she was so mixed up, and so mad at the frog, she even hated to look at him. All she could do was to do nothing. And that sure wasn't easy. But she found out that when she did nothing, at least the frog didn't do any worse, and the house was quieter without her nagging all the time. He still acted ugly, and if she even said *hello,* he would say, "There you go, nagging again!" But the lump she had been carrying around somewhere in her chest started to go away little by little. The day finally came when the prince came in drunk, and she looked up from what she was doing and smiled and said, "Hi, prince," and meant it.

"Go to hell," said the prince.

"Maybe later," she said, "but right now I thought I would go to the movies. Would you like to go?"

"Drop dead," answered the frog.

● ● ● ● ● ● ● ● ● ●

"I'm leaving you something in the oven for your supper," she said. "I hope you will feel better soon." And she went.

Things are Better
It would be nice to be able to say that after that everything was just fine, and that the frog changed, because she changed, and they lived happily ever after. They're still together, but both of them are pretty lonely. Her heart just aches when she looks at him, because she remembers what a prince he was, and she knows how he must hate being a frog. She can tell that he is glad she's not squeezing the stuffing out of him all the time. When he is sick and miserable it makes him mad to see her singing and smiling, and doing what she wants to whether he goes with her or not.

Sometimes he says to himself and to her and to anybody else who will listen, "You just don't give a damn, do you?"

But she does give a damn, and she tries to show him that she does. She knows she can't keep him from being a frog, but she has learned that there are frogs who have turned back into princes. He could, if he really wanted to badly enough.

He hasn't so far—but things are better—and she has hardly any warts.

LOVE

Rare Insight

I had never loved myself. Yet failing this, I tried to love an alcoholic. I didn't see it at the time but, in retrospect, I wonder if I didn't feel so alienated from myself that I'd hoped to destroy myself through the alcoholic and then neatly pin the blame on him.

I didn't know how to live and let live, how to treat people

• • • • • • • • • •

as persons. To me they were things to be manipulated in a system of emotional barter and blackmail which I used to gain security, approval and satisfactions. Although I self-righteously called it *give and take,* it amounted to *kill or be killed.*

After a short period of sobriety, my husband returned to drinking and ended our relationship. I was forced to look into those dark corners I'd never seen before. With the help of the program, I realized that in order to love and respect myself, I would have to admit that I'd been exploiting my husband. My only honest choice was to let him go.

It's ironic, but in letting go, I have finally learned an emotionally comfortable, mature way to love. By releasing each other with love, we have given each other all the help we could give. I believe it is the first act of real love I have ever made.

A Lesson in Compassion

My children and I thought that when my spouse stopped drinking, life would really be great. He would go places with us, and he wouldn't be grouchy from hangovers anymore. Were we in for a surprise!

He still didn't go with us—he went to AA meetings instead and he was grouchier than ever. The kids couldn't seem to understand when I told them their father was grouchy because his body was being denied the alcohol it had become accustomed to.

Then I got an idea. I had the children pick out their favorite snack. Whatever it was, they weren't to have any for one week. They were tempted many times, and I then gently reminded them that this was how it was for their father. We all learned a lesson in compassion.

● ● ● ● ● ● ● ● ● ●

Love Unites Us In Common Purpose

*I*t occurred to me that February, the month of love, high-lighted by Saint Valentine's Day on the 14th, has always been associated with romantic love, physical and emotional love be-tween two people. The greeting cards are filled with hearts, sometimes arrow-pierced, and flowers, and irresistibly beauti-ful young people. This is touching in its way, especially for those *in love*.

Love, in our fellowship, is a far broader concept. It is, in-deed, a universal feeling embracing all of troubled mankind. In learning to love in this way, we learn to accept our fellow-man without fault-finding judgments, without a holier-than-thou attitude, and with compassion. In Al-Anon, we become aware of the love of God for us and for all humanity, and, in our little limited human way, we try to emulate it.

Such love is giving, giving freely of ourselves and whatever help we can provide for those who are still suffering the dis-tresses of living with the problem of alcoholism. Best of all, we learn to love and forgive ourselves, to have patience with our errors and to renew our efforts to overcome them.

This is the kind of love that unites us in a common pur-pose. As our First Tradition says: "Personal progress for the greatest number depends upon unity" and unity depends upon mutual love and acceptance. To quote Pierre Teilhard de Chardin, "Love alone is capable of uniting living beings in such a way as to complete and fulfill them."

● ● ● ● ● ● ● ● ● ●

A Legacy of Love

*I*n Al-Anon, the opportunities to love and be loved are endless. One way to show love is to reach out to someone in need and to listen. More difficult and yet even more important is to love and listen to myself. It's in those still, quiet moments that the Higher Power speaks. When I don't listen, the static of life takes over.

At first, although I could feel the love of others, the concept of a loving Higher Power was hard for me to accept. During the many dark days and nights of alcoholism, I'd felt God had abandoned me. Although the signs of His love were everywhere, I couldn't see them: the gift of life, my health, two lovely daughters, a gentle, kind husband.

Coping with alcoholism has helped to make us strong. When the stormy years ended, the love we received from AA and Al-Anon showed us how to heal our bruises, mend the damage, and lead fruitful, dignified lives.

When my Higher Power takes back my life, I probably won't leave many personal possessions or much wealth behind. I would rather know that I have touched the spirit of others and helped them to enrich their lives. Then my legacy would be one of love. The love that has sustained me in my life would continue to live and manifest itself in others.

● ● ● ● ● ● ● ● ● ●

Love—Al-Anon's Secret Formula

*P*rofessionals in the field of alcoholism often study AA and Al-Anon, to see if they can find out what makes our groups so successful. They apply scientific principles to try to analyze and discover the secret, but it always seems to elude them.

Professionals in other fields, having seen the great good that has come from our fellowships, try to apply the group concept in *therapeutic communities, extended families,* or *redemptive groups.* But these seem to lack that certain something that makes AA and Al-Anon so effective.

Why do our groups work where so many have failed? Is it our basic belief in a Higher Power and surrender of our lives to His will? Is it the common bond of suffering? Is it our Traditions? The peer approach? The group concept? I'm sure it's all of these. But I don't think any of them would work without love.

It is love that makes the frightened, ashamed newcomer feel welcome; that causes us to encourage each other's gains, no matter how small, and tolerate each other's failings, no matter how glaring. It is love that prompts the commitment we make to each other, to be there when we are needed. What else but love would make a person share home and food and time for the sheer pleasure of it? What else but love would make us feel that we have received when we have given, that we have been helped when we have helped?

Someone once said that emotional illness is the fear or conviction that we are not lovable. Not believing that we will be loved for ourselves, we try to take care of our need for love in various destructive or unproductive ways: buying friendship with gifts, favors, agreeableness; conforming; being perfec-

• • • • • • • • • • •

tionists or acting helpless; making people feel sorry for us or, certain of rejection, we reject first, assuming a critical, offensive attitude. Avoiding intimacy, and the loneliness that results from that isolation, are preferred to the pain of rejection.

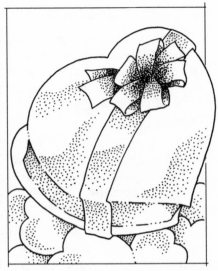

But Al-Anon, with its sheltering cloak of warmth, acceptance and caring, helps us to shed our facades and to say *I'm afraid.* We learn to share ourselves and take risks. We learn to invest feelings in people once again. Accepted by others before we accept ourselves, forgiven before we forgive ourselves, loved before we feel lovable, we are reborn to a joyous, beautiful life.

A Message Of Love

Valentine's Day seems appropriate for an installment payment. No absolutely authentic reasons are attributed to its origin. But many of us are drawn to it as a time of giving small gifts and sending loving greetings to dear ones. Since the Al-Anon program heads the list of many gifts given me, I'd like to send to all of you these two Valentine remembrances. You may not need them as much as I, but please don't forget them. Two things seem most important to me. One does not absorb this program by osmosis, at least initially. It takes work, thought and persistence to make it our own. We need to practice Al-Anon principles in all our affairs, diligently, until the right methods of handling difficulties become automatic. Our reactions change to conditioned reflexes; they no longer

• • • • • • • • • •

are impulsive manifestations of fear, disgust and impatience.

The other idea concerns Twelfth-Step work, part of which is sponsoring others. When working with the sponsored, and also when speaking to groups, we should be careful, neither to present an image of superiority nor to have had the very worst of problems.

Personally, I had a severe and prolonged struggle with accepting the First Step. It could truthfully be called my five years war. But honest appraisal shows that my problem was not worse than others. The basic cause was my inability to accept powerlessness. My stubborn belief in finding my own solution kept me in turmoil.

Others, perhaps with more difficulties than mine, found help and serenity much sooner than I. But we can all find both if we persist with open minds and determination.

So, my Valentine to all of you comes with a great deal of love in a few words: "Keep on keeping on." And as someone said so cogently: "What we don't learn by studying the Steps we learn by living them."

SELF-ACCEPTANCE

Key To Sanity—Self-acceptance

My husband has been sober these past two and a half years, and is basically a kind and easy-to-get-along-with person. My kids are sweeties. Yet I have found myself in a habit of resentful thinking—*oh they don't care what I cook—he's so selfish—if they'd only listen to me—it's your fault*—etc. Sometimes I express this; usually I judge it, find it wrong, don't want to blow my *sainted mother* image, so I bottle it up to sneak out in mean, subtle, sick little ways. I have found myself with a self-perpetuating mental illness as bad as alcoholism. My cycle: feel resentful and hateful toward my family; feel guilty and self-hateful for feeling that way; feel sorry for myself; try to express love and cheerfulness; but can't really because I feel self-hatred and it blocks the flow of love; feel more guilt and self-hate, etc.

So for me, a key has been self-acceptance. I've read so many Al-Anon, AA and psychology books that it's beginning to seep through to my moralistic little self that it is acceptable and human to feel angry, tired or lazy; and that I can ask for help, love, affection, appreciation; that it's okay to feel frustrated when my needs aren't being fulfilled. In other words, it's okay to be human. That doesn't mean I let my negative human side run me. I just accept it so I can deal with it. And realize that some of my basic desires are needs, that they are good, and ought to be met. Self-acceptance seems to me to be a necessary first step to accepting others, and both are necessary for any kind of real communication and love. My self-judging and self-loathing run deep, back to six or seven years of age or maybe younger, and I don't expect to get over these bad habits in a day. But I feel I'm heading in the right direction and I no longer feel crucified by my own guilt.

Shame and Strain—Prelude To Membership

We Al-Anon members talk a lot about spiritual growth and about maturing in the program. This is quite natural. Many of us come by Al-Anon Family Groups spiritually bankrupt and as unable to deal with our lives and problems as lost children trying to find their way in a dark and alien forest.

None of us went astray deliberately. Strain played a most important part. Shame and disappointment added their not inconsiderable weight. Most of all, ignorance and a sense of being alone in a hostile world kept us concentrated and occupied with situations Al-Anon later taught us to handle competently and serenely.

• • • • • • • • • •

The strain was real; we seldom knew from one day to another when a disagreeable situation would progress from bad to a thousand times worse. Too many times we relied upon promises of improvement only to find them unfulfilled, because they came from the alcoholic's desire to get us off his back. We learned to discount everything. We had not yet learned that alcoholism is a disease now ranked the number two public health problem in the United States, and a major one in most, or many, other countries.

Neither had we yet learned we were not responsible to the disease. We felt we had failed our partners when they continued to drink to excess. We too, like our neighbors, looked upon drunkenness as something to be hidden, so we shut ourselves in upon ourselves to carry the burden alone.

Self-pity we had in plenty. And many reveled in it until they learned in Al-Anon that self-pity is what John W. Gardner described as "easily the most destructive of the non-pharmaceutical narcotics; it is addictive, gives momentary pleasure and separates the victim from reality."

So it was, after a time in the Al-Anon program, that we learned people are important. The well-known popular song, *People Who Need People Are The Luckiest People in the World* began to make more sense to us. From shunning others, shutting them out, we learned to relate to them, to meet their needs either actively by showing them how they will grow by helping others, or passively by just listening to their troubles. Either way we lessened their burdens and took part in their return to the everyday world.

This acknowledgment of our role in other peoples' lives and problems was doubly important. Our help bolstered the other person's courage, showed them how to climb up from a pit of despair. It also widened our own horizons, served to show us our own lapses and lacks. When we realized that barricading ourselves behind high walls could only make us stop growing

• • • • • • • • • • •

and keep us untouchable and alone, we made extra efforts to rejoin our fellowmen.

We found our own problems dwindled as we learned how to handle them. We learned to distinguish where we could and should help others. We learned how to become, or to become again, the people we were originally meant to be, spiritually oriented and capable of maturing healthily and happily.

<u>Self-Esteem</u>

Convinced I Wasn't A Man

I didn't expect Al-Anon to change me or my emotions; I only hoped somehow to make my life more tolerable. I believed I was inferior and without peers, and never imagined I could feel differently.

Life had been an endless treadmill of putting up a front to gain the approval of others, always fearing they'd see through me and think, *what a nothing.*

My wife's alcoholism convinced me I wasn't a man, for had I been, I would have been able to make her happy. Deep feelings of guilt, resentment, frustration and loneliness made my life a burden.

I entered an all-woman Al-Anon group whose members rallied and turned their sympathetic attention toward me. Eventually, I was able to accept the truth that I could change. I am responsible for myself. Freedom from ill-will towards others is wonderful. Being able to say *I love you* is an unexpected gift.

I worry about leaving an unhappy wife to attend two meetings a week, but feel less guilty about it. I know she must find her own happiness.

● ● ● ● ● ● ● ● ● ●

Action is the key to the positive attitudes I desire. I pray for love and gratitude. With faith in my Higher Power, I act as if I had them, and suddenly realize they are there, deep within.

I see miracles at every meeting I attend, but can only understand the one that is happening to me.

Stands By Principles

I cannot survive without my program and meetings. I know I am well only one day at a time because I can quickly take over my family's lives unless I apply the program to all my living.

My deterioration was much greater after my husband's sobriety than before, and I did a lot of damage during my son's drinking. It was only when I was able to *Let Go and Let God* and apply the other principles of our program that my son became sober.

I have learned to look at myself, to like and respect the person I am, and to stand by my principles instead of being controlled by other people's ideas and demands. Sometimes I'd be appalled at the situations I'd allowed myself to get into, but thanks to the program I no longer have to hide in shame.

I'm Good To Myself

I am responsible for the way I feel. It's up to me to find happiness. It helps to treat myself like a good friend. Many of my childhood values had to be updated because I'd outgrown them. I don't listen to character assassinations—mine or anyone else's.

I must allow others their feelings. If my husband and children are upset, it's not necessarily my fault. I must back off

● ● ● ● ● ● ● ● ● ●

and allow others to find the way to victory over themselves.

I don't accept guilt, take on blame, or act out someone else's anger. I have enough of my own to deal with.

I am good to myself. I share my deep feelings, good and bad, with others. I stay close to God, let go, and accept the results. He certainly doesn't need me to make His miracles. I talk nicely to myself and pat myself on the back when I do what's right but difficult. I do things for others, sometimes anonymously. I fix my hair, take a bubble bath, watch my diet, visit my neighbor with a plate of cookies, tell my girls I'm glad they're my daughters, phone someone I haven't heard from in a long time. All this I do to like myself better.

Freedom—Our Precious Heritage

Not too many years ago I considered myself a prisoner in my own home. I didn't feel free to do anything just because I wanted to; everything was geared to the needs and desires of my children and husband. All of my feelings and wishes were subordinate to theirs. I played the part of the martyr very well, silent and long-suffering. Silent, because I didn't feel free to speak up for fear my temperamental alcoholic would explode. I had let myself become a doormat and wallowed in resentment and self-pity. I wore myself out trying to be the perfect mother, wife and housekeeper, and of course had no free time to spend on myself.

The turning point came about five years ago when the two older children had grown and left home and our littlest one was in school all day. Suddenly, I had time on my hands, time I didn't know what to do with because I still didn't know how to be good to myself. I spent the days worrying about the children, and continually resentful of my husband. During the drinking days when things had been really rough, I'd always taken the children and left because I didn't know how to cope

● ● ● ● ● ● ● ● ● ●

with the problem. Now I found myself wanting to escape from this unhappy marriage again, but I knew I couldn't separate our little son from his daddy whom he has never seen take a drink, because they are inseparable.

I bought a *One Day At A Time In Al-Anon* book and read it from cover to cover. In it I read that if we are not happy with our situation and yet not ready to make a break, we had better get busy and work to change the situation, but we start by changing ourselves. I also read that Al-Anon is a way to personal freedom. When I read that, I thought, *Oh yeah? How?* and threw the book across the room. Then I knew how Lois felt when she threw her shoe at Bill. Of course, after a time I picked up the book and reread it because I wanted desperately to find out how to obtain that personal freedom for myself.

The first thing I learned was that I had to pay a price. Like everything else that is worth having, freedom is not free. The price is acceptance. The First Step had come easy. I knew I couldn't control the alcoholic's drinking. I accepted that. The part that came hard was accepting that I couldn't control what he said or did.

Since he had been sober for quite sometime, I expected him to be a new man, to be rid of his character defects. This was unrealistic. Sobriety is but the first step in building a good life, and he has the right and obligation to work on his defects in his own way, without any directions from me. This was the hardest part of all, accepting that I couldn't change anyone but myself. I struggled with this for quite some time before I realized that this acceptance could give me my freedom—freedom to be me and freedom to be good to myself. Now I take time for myself every day, even if it's just for a few moments of relaxing with a good book. I feel free to go places and do the things I want to do.

I can remember when my husband controlled the money. I resented his keeping ten dollars a week for his spending money, while I often had to ask him for a quarter to put in the Al-Anon basket. Why did I live under these conditions? Because I hadn't yet learned to assert myself. I had no self-confidence, no feeling of self-worth. I had to learn to like myself. Finally, I came to realize that I, too, am a person. I have the right to a happy, contented life. I don't have to live in the shadow of a domineering spouse. I can be me. I have found many treasures in Al-Anon, but personal freedom is the greatest.

SELF-KNOWLEDGE

Too Much Of A Good Thing

I came into Al-Anon because my husband wanted me to—no other reason. I believed I was superior to people in AA and Al-Anon. I thought *with a little self-control, these people wouldn't be in the degrading condition they're in now.* I had no faults; my irrational behavior was due to my husband's problem.

Even with this attitude, I continued to go to meetings, never sharing. Finally, I became aware of myself and my life and began to change.

• • • • • • • • • •

I became active in my group and district, and I began to work with newcomers. I had never been so fulfilled.

Our group split, but we continued to get more new people every week. Several of them asked me to sponsor them. I was elated—I was very *involved.*

Before I realized it, I was on the phone every day and most evenings. My house was going to pot, my children were unattended, and my husband was getting very upset. I rationalized by saying *this is my job in Al-Anon; these people need me.*

I found myself in a state of anxiety most of the time. Then my bubble burst. A girl I was sponsoring began to see me as a human being—not her Higher Power. People in the group started complaining about members trying to manipulate and control others. Membership fell off from twenty to four or five. Anonymity was being broken.

With time and help from our Higher Power things will change. I've learned a painful lesson from all this:

1. Twelfth-Step work doesn't mean giving everything to everyone. No person is totally responsible for a group and its members.

2. Anonymity should always be uppermost in my mind, especially when dealing with close personal relationships.

3. Detachment should be practiced toward everyone, not just the alcoholic.

I took a thorough inventory and realized what has to come first in my life: my Al-Anon program for me, my husband and my children, and then carrying the message, in that order.

My good intentions, without the proper Al-Anon guidelines, caused me and others a lot of harm. I'm slowly coming out of the shock of what happened to me and my group. I'm grateful to my Higher Power and my group for giving me the aware-

● ● ● ● ● ● ● ● ● ●

ness I needed. I am convinced now that I will never be too well for Al-Anon because every day I am learning more about myself.

On Being Real—Some Really Good Thoughts

*I*t goes without saying that we walk the walk as well as talk the talk for the sake of the newcomers who look to us as examples; but even more, we need to be real for our own sakes. We cannot feel one way on the inside and try to be another person on the outside without having this dichotomy take its emotional toll. This inner-outer conflict sometimes shows itself in illness, sometimes in depression, but always there is the frustration of being unable to express what we really are. And I can only know as much of myself as I am able to express to you.

I am not being real if I pretend I am never angry or depressed or fearful. The program teaches me to admit to the feeling, recognize it, name it—*I am angry!*—and decide how to handle it. Feelings in themselves are neither good nor bad and saying *I shouldn't* feel a certain way is unrealistic.

I am not being real if I pretend that, because I have been in the program many years, I no longer have times of tension and anxiety, times of real need. I've been this route and it leads nowhere. When I hurt, I *holler* for help. On the other hand, it would be denying the power of God in my life if I claimed that nothing had changed or improved in the last twelve years. There have been enormous improvements and changes; I am counting on there being many more.

Being real does not mean that I have to reveal all my innermost self to everyone I meet; it does mean that however much of myself I choose to share must be genuine, my real self. Being real means living in reality.

Living in reality does not mean being negative. The worst

• • • • • • • • • •

that could happen rarely did. Surely there has been more good than bad in our lives. It's a *cop-out* to voice the negative constantly and say we are just being realistic; that isn't accurate. It is belied by the facts.

Being real does not mean releasing hostility under the guise of honesty. If I must speak some unpleasant truth in love, I must be very sure that circumstances warrant my doing so. And if doing so gives me the slightest bit of pleasure, I had better look to my motives again.

My being genuine does not depend on the realness or phoniness of others. I am responsible only for keeping my own insides and outsides matching. I can risk being my real self because I am no longer dependent on the approval of others. My opinion of me no longer depends on their opinion of me. When it did, I could not let many people see who I really am.

And because you have loved me back to life, I have become increasingly able to leave myself open and vulnerable, knowing that my relationship with God can be no better than my relationship with His children.

Not What She Wants To Be

*B*efore Al-Anon I felt inferior, rejected, lonely and unloved. I had difficulty expressing my love for others and still do. I nagged, could never let well-enough alone, was spiteful. My troubles were so much on my mind that even when I went to church, I couldn't hear what was being said.

In Al-Anon I am gradually learning to come out of my cocoon and to share. Now I know that it's impossible to love others unless we love ourselves. I no longer have to carry anyone else's burdens. I depend on Al-Anon for my soul food. Each time someone shares with me, it helps me to grow, and I grow when I share with others, too. I'm not what I want to

● ● ● ● ● ● ● ● ● ● ●

be, I'm not what I'm going to be, but I'm the best me I can
be today.

Self-knowledge Leads To Humility

I am a priest engaged in teaching college students and giving spiritual direction to other priests. My work has often
brought me into contact with the problems of alcoholism in
my priest friends and in my students. One of my AA associ-
ates urged me to go to Al-Anon. I decided to try it, even though
I felt there wasn't much to learn since I had already read
much about alcoholism, had listened to lectures and the like.

Surprise! I found that Al-Anon taught me to understand
myself. Knowledge of self is the foundation of true humility.
And knowledge of myself is the key to my own dealings with
friends caught up in the disease of alcoholism.

The past seven months of Al-Anon have brought about a
remarkable development: I seem to have gained more self-
knowledge this year than in all the years before. AA and Al-
Anon literature (especially ODAT) have given me many insights
into myself and others. But the greatest help has been the
living experience of sharing with a fine group of friends. The
mutual support of friends in our program is more than just
words. The words seem to take on meaning beyond themselves
when they come from men and women who share with one
another the joys, the complexities, the sorrows and the challenges of life.

• • • • • • • • • •

Finding The Right Direction

*P*eople often come into Al-
Anon expecting to find specific answers to specific
problems. That's not the way
it works, but they may find
the most helpful suggestion
in the closing statement
which urges newcomers to
talk things over, reason
things out with someone
else. This method helps us
find solutions because we in
Al-Anon share our experi-
ence, strength and hope.

It can be compared to the boatman navigating in a fog. The
waves will ring the buoy bell and tell him which direction to
take. We who are at one time or another trapped in the fog
of confusion, are making waves by talking things over with
someone else. One of these waves will ring the *buoy bell* for us.

Knowledge of the sea helps the boatman recognize the true
sound of the bell and know which is the right direction to
take. Knowledge of ourselves and our problems helps us recognize the path to follow to find our way out of the confusion.

So talk things over and reason things out. You will find
solutions which lead to serenity. I have, and so have thou-
sands of others who rely on Al-Anon for spiritual help.

• • • • • • • • • •

Other Side Of Coin

*T*his is from a former compulsive talker and monopolizer. My life was totally unmanageable. I was angry, loud and full of self-pity. Who could love that? I wouldn't let you, anyway.

After studying and trying to work my program, I could talk good Al-Anon and it made me feel better. No one listened to me at home. After a while, I sensed a hostile feeling from the group. Then I realized that if I wanted to fit in, I would have to change.

I'd promised myself to listen at meetings but would always blow it and then feel guilty. Try as I might, I couldn't stop talking. One day, a male member said, "Arlene, let the new girl say something." I was angry, but it helped. Others also helped by saying things like *what you say is good, but I would like to hear from so and so.*

I am still irritated and find it hard to keep quiet when I run across people who take up precious meeting time with small talk, or who never read the literature.

You can help the compulsive talker by loving her, giving her a job, inviting her for coffee. What do we gain by loving only the lovable?

An Independent Person Learns To Accept Help

*I'*ve always been proud of my independence. However, I recently became aware that I'd carried this character trait too far. As with any good thing, it's not good when it's overdone. Although always ready to help others, I never liked to ask others to do me a favor. I didn't want to burden them. I didn't want people to find me annoying. I didn't want to suffer the pain of being turned down or let down when I really needed

• • • • • • • • • •

help. I was afraid people wouldn't want me, afraid they wouldn't like me, afraid they'd reject me. Recently, a severe illness which required hospitalization put me in the position of having to become totally dependent on others. I had no choice but to accept their help. I learned so very much from what happened:

1. People enjoyed doing things for me; it made them feel important, needed. The message they'd been getting from my independent behavior was, *I don't need you* or *I don't trust you,* not at all what I'd been trying to say!

2. By seldom asking for or accepting help from others, I'd been unconsciously trying to tell myself that I was better, stronger than they. Being placed in a totally helpless position made me realize that my lovableness didn't depend solely on my being the rescuer. The rescued person is also lovable.

Why hadn't that occurred to me even though I loved the people I helped, and got genuine enjoyment and fulfillment from helping them? Could it be I was the one who was secretly annoyed at the demands placed upon me, but was getting satisfaction out of being the martyr? Could it be I was uncomfortable with accepting from others because I didn't want to have to be beholden—called upon to help when I really didn't want to, and then doing it out of a sense of obligation and debt?

There's a lot to be said for being flat on your back, unable even to turn over by yourself. The discipline of self-examination and meditation learned in Al-Anon served me well then. I asked myself those difficult questions and got to know myself and others a little better. I realized that, in addition to being an expression of my care and concern for others, my independence and helpfulness was a cover-up for my own feelings of inadequacy. My self-confidence and feelings of self-worth weren't quite what I thought they were.

Once I relaxed about having to let others wash me and

• • • • • • • • • •

take care of my basic needs, I began to be truly nourished by their love and concern. I learned that I could trust others with my welfare, that I wouldn't be let down or rejected for my helplessness. And I learned that the world could and would go on without me. My husband and children missed me, and so did my co-workers. But they managed. People pitched in and the work got done.

I don't know whether the lessons we learn this way make permanent changes in our behavior. I suspect we need constant vigilance not to fall back into old behavior patterns. But I do know that I've had another real example of the beauty and wisdom of this program. With the help of our Higher Power, we can use even bad situations to bring about good results.

At the time, I couldn't see how any good could possibly come from my illness. As I look back, the lessons I learned in compassion and love, the gratitude and humility I acquired, and the self-awareness I gained were well worth the price.

I'm better now, and back to my regular routine. I hope if I ever again feel uncomfortable about having to ask for or accept help, that this recent experience will be a vivid reminder that such independence is really arrogance. Allowing others to express their love and concern for me can be one of the most valuable gifts I can give them.

SERENITY

Life With And Without

I once heard a member say that to her, serenity is life without: without turmoil, without anger, without dissension. Remembering that I once felt the same way, I didn't leap to my feet to disagree, but I did sit there thinking, *no, serenity is life WITH!* It's life with turmoil and trouble and all the other

• • • • • • • • • •

ills to which flesh is heir, but it is also life with a Power greater than ourselves, with a set of tools with which to tackle problems, with a community of people who give us emotional support and remind us of what we believe. Serenity is not freedom from the storm but peace amid the storm; not escape from conflict but inner stability within the conflict.

Hit Bottom And Found Peace

After thirty years of domination, confusion, tears and heartbreak, I found Al-Anon. All my life I'd had an emptiness in my soul and never knew what I was looking for. I have found it in Al-Anon and in my Higher Power.

It has been three years since I joined Al-Anon. One of my four children has joined me in the program. The others find it hard to understand some of the changes they see in me, especially my refusal to get back on the merry-go-round.

Three years ago, I was ready to give up. I never wanted to see the light of morning come. I was going down and couldn't stop myself. I just didn't care anymore. The means to take my life were right in my purse, but I cried out *God, help me, I'm going down.* I reached for the telephone and called an Al-Anon member who asked me to come to her home. I did. She and another woman talked to me for six hours. They smiled and looked at me with love I'd never seen before. They knew my hell and they didn't try to talk me out of killing myself, but they didn't pity me, either. All they said was, "Will you give us a chance to help you? Just come to our meetings and listen."

I've never been happier about anything I've ever done. Day by day I've discovered it is wonderful to be alive. I've found friends, people who understand. I've learned to pray and say *stay with me, Lord.* Sometimes it works so well it scares me.

One day my husband was yelling at me as usual. He could

• • • • • • • • • •

get me so upset I couldn't even pick up a cup. My insides were shaking so much I couldn't say a word. All of a sudden, the warmest feeling came over me. It started in my head and went down through my whole body. My stomach relaxed; even my legs stopped shaking. I could talk. No one had to tell me what happened. I believe it was my spiritual awakening. Even my husband saw the change in me. He stopped yelling and said, "Mama, are you okay?" I looked at him and smiled because it was the most wonderful feeling I'd ever had and I said, "I have found peace of mind. You can't hurt me any more."

And it's true. Oh, I'm not saying it all stopped right then and there. My husband still drinks and yells at me, but I don't try to defend myself anymore. I don't have to. I'm not afraid.

SPONSORSHIP

The Frustrations And Joys Of Sponsorship

The main way my Higher Power guides me is through other people, and sometimes I surrender enough so that He can use me as a guide for someone else. We give guidance to each other, and receive it from each other, when we talk at meetings and when we talk personally, in the letters we write and the lives we live. I couldn't make it on a day-to-day basis without the loving guidance of several people, and I surely could not grow much in the program without being allowed to give loving guidance to those who come my way.

Inevitably there are problems. I know I caused some to the people who guided me, and others have assuredly caused me some. Here are a few:

1. There are those who really don't want to get well. Changing is painful, allowing others to change is painful, insight

is painful, and they'd rather just talk about it. These are the ones who do nothing the program suggests, yet continue to bewail their lot and wonder why things don't get better.

2. Then there are the *shoppers*. These people go from sponsor to sponsor or friend to friend, never staying with one person long enough to get anything accomplished. Sometimes it's because they can't take the rigorous honesty the program talks about. Sometimes they are hunting someone who will tell them only what they want to hear. Sometimes they are unable to let anyone come close to them. Then they start over with someone else.

3. There are those who not only tell everyone they see what you've said to them, but they misquote.

4. There are those who want back door Al-Anon. They want many long, private consultations, but no meetings, thank you. If we tolerate this, I guess we deserve it.

5. Then there are those who play *yes, but.* They build their ego by insisting that their problem is worse than anyone else's, the program can't possibly help it, and God can't possibly handle it.

Ah, but there are those who come into our lives like gifts from God! They listen, they try, they get up when they fall down, they regard us as people who have been in the program a little longer than they, perhaps, but not as saints. They enrich our own convictions by letting us see the principles newly applied and newly practiced. They replenish us, rather than drain us. They're what it's all about!

• • • • • • • • • •

Coping With Slips

I have been in Al-Anon 10-12 years. I joined when my husband was actively drinking. Since then he has embraced AA, but has had many slips as well as beautiful sobriety.

After a fairly long spell of sobriety, he recently had another slip. I immediately called my sponsor. We never outgrow our need for a sponsor—someone who, over the years, gets to know us better than we know ourselves.

Telling her about what was happening helped me get my head on straight. After getting rid of the garbage—*do I have to look forward to this for the rest of my life?* and *do I want to do something about it?*—I was able to settle peacefully into the routine of living with an active problem.

My sponsor helped me to face what was happening by letting me talk about it and set the stage for my adjustment to it by reminding me to detach emotionally. I was reminded my reaction probably would be quite different if he were having a relapse from a heart condition.

Thankfully, the slip only lasted a week. During that time, I managed to not react, and was able to treat him with compassion. Thank God for Al-Anon.

• • • • • • • • • •

• • • • • • • • • •

Slogans and The Serenity Prayer

As a result of daily reading, thinking about the slogans, measuring my actions and decisions against the standards of the Serenity Prayer, and accepting guidance from my Higher Power, I have recently experienced the thrill of accomplishment.

EASY DOES IT

Discussion Of Easy Does It

*T*his has always been my favorite slogan around the holidays because it helps me to enjoy the festivities. I have a tendency to pack each day, week and month of the year with activity. I like being busy and thrive on such a schedule. But when the holidays roll around, with all the extra activities—baking, decorating, shopping, wrapping, card-sending, entertaining, etc., I find I'm suddenly overwhelmed.

Without this slogan to remind me to slow down, I start over-working, rushing, getting irritable, and before I know it, I'm exhausted. *Easy Does It* reminds me I don't have to do everything in one day, that I must be good to myself. If I'm going to add five activities to my calendar for December, I'd better see what I can do about slowing down in other areas. Demanding more of myself than I can comfortably accomplish is a sure recipe for feelings of frustration, failure and depression.

Those of us who push ourselves tend to be just as demanding of others; but I've yet to find anyone who likes to be pushed. I must constantly be on my guard to allow others to grow at their own rate, not mine. Just because I want to get so many things done in one day, I have no right to demand that others around me adopt my standards and goals. I used

• • • • • • • • • •

to get so irritated at this. I would set out with a list of ob-
jectives for the day, and then get angry when those around
me balked and were uncooperative. I'd forgotten that I haven't
the right to plan anyone's life but my own. If I choose to over-
work, that's my problem. I can't blame my tiredness on someone else's decision to take it easy. I can make the same decision,
if I choose.

Continuing Emotional Problems

*D*uring his recovery my husband experienced severe emotional problems that required hospitalization, time away from
work, and a demotion. Although I was truly trying to practice
my program, I continued to be miserable.

An experienced Al-Anon member listened to me talk about
this problem for a few minutes, then politely interrupted me
and said, "Honey, you haven't released this problem." Although
the words stung, they continued to echo in my head for days.
I could see that I was trying to control the situation, being
too helpful and offering too many suggestions.

I had to realize I can't fix everything and I don't have to
do something about every situation. *Easy Does It* is an important slogan for me. Change is painful, but I find comfort
in applying the First Step to all problems.

Six months have now passed since my husband's hospitalization. He has made progress by leaps and bounds. Our
relationship is better than ever.

Should new problems arise that I can't handle, I will try
to talk about my feelings with someone who, I hope, will be
as honest with me as this friend was.

● ● ● ● ● ● ● ● ● ●

First Things First

First Things First

We have been married for 19 years. The drinking has been a problem for 18 years, although my husband has been in and out of AA for the past 12 years. He has lost many jobs and has been hospitalized several times, but never has found permanent sobriety.

I have worked for 17 years. I tried quitting my job and following him to areas that looked greener. But in the end, he lost his job and we were forced to go on welfare. My children were 5 years and 6 months-old then. That was when I found Al-Anon.

I learned to put *First Things First.* To me, that means my children's welfare. I decided to return to work. Luckily, I can earn enough to support the family. However, I do not share my bank account and check book with my husband.

He is out of work off and on and continues to live at home. However, I realize I can't compare his effort at AA to anyone else's. Not everyone sobers up because someone hurried up a crisis.

It's important, in situations like ours, to do what will be of greatest benefit to all family members. I am grateful I can provide the necessities of life. When my husband is out of town working, he provides for himself. I hope someday he will find sobriety and a real joy for living, God willing.

• • • • • • • • • •

Discussion Of First Things First

First Things First helps me in my everyday routine, especially around the holidays, or busy times when there seems to be far more to do than there is time to do it. Doing what must be done first, and then what's next in importance, and so on, brings such an orderliness, such an unhurried feeling to my day. Before I know it, I've accomplished much more than I thought I could, certainly much more than if I'd started five things at once and finished none of them.

This slogan has had an even deeper effect on my life than that—it has changed my entire sense of values. Things that used to seem so important to me seem much less so now. Before Al-Anon, the thing that came first in my life—the need that guided most of my actions—was the desire for the affection and admiration of others. Because I didn't have a good opinion of myself, I was concerned with what others thought of me, and any kind of disapproval or rejection made me uncomfortable. If others liked me, then I felt good about myself; if they disliked me or criticized me, I felt compelled to change to please them. My opinion of myself depended entirely on others. Being married to an alcoholic who was over-critical, and who blamed me for his drinking, didn't do much for my self-image. No matter how hard I tried to please, it seemed I never could.

Appearances mattered a great deal, too. I tried to impress those around me—my parents, my family, my friends and neighbors—by doing everything perfectly: keeping house, taking care of the children, cooking, etc. I was always terribly self-conscious because I was terrified of looking like an incompetent. That was such an awful constriction. I was afraid to speak, for fear of sounding silly; afraid to try something new for fear of failing; afraid to relax and enjoy myself for fear of looking foolish. It never occurred to me that people are un-

• • • • • • • • • •

comfortable with apparent perfection in others; there's something awfully prissy, rigid and forbidding about someone who is always right, efficient and correct. It never occurred to me that my husband's perception of me wasn't accurate, or that I didn't have to live up to other people's expectations. Trying so hard to win their admiration by being perfect, I robbed myself of their friendship by preventing them from knowing the real me. It appeared as though I was setting myself apart and above; too good to have failings and weaknesses the way they did. No wonder I was lonely. But I didn't see it then the way I do now.

Today I realize that, instead of putting the opinions of others first, I must work on improving my own feelings of self-worth. As long as I feel like a truly worthwhile person, I can be less concerned with what others think.

Not satisfied with admiration alone, I sought affection, too. I thought mistakenly, that by always putting the wishes of others first, I would win their love. I carried this *unselfishness* to an extreme, until I was a self-made martyr, a doormat. I didn't realize that in sacrificing my own welfare, I was arousing guilt feelings in those I was *helping*. I couldn't understand it when, instead of being grateful, they took even more advantage of me. Then the resentments came, and the self-pity. I didn't realize that people only do to us what we allow them to do.

Now, of course, I consider my own welfare. If something is good for me, it probably is good for the rest of my family, too. This is a general principle, but one that has brought me many rewards. It has helped me to make difficult decisions, to develop myself as a person, and to achieve a degree of integrity I never had before.

Thank God for Al-Anon, where I finally developed a sense of values that makes sense: *first things first*; people are more important than things; what I think of myself is more impor-

• • • • • • • • • • •

tant to me than what someone else thinks of me; my welfare must come first; my integrity is worth the price I pay for it.

HOW IMPORANT IS IT?

Discussion Of How Important Is It

*T*his slogan helps me every day. I work with some volatile people who seem to be in a constant state of panic. They take on too many responsibilities, operate on impossibly tight schedules, and get upset, erupting like volcanos, when unexpected things come along. They can't bend, and they carry their frustration with them wherever they go. They're in too much of a hurry to be considerate.

By repeating *How Important Is It* to myself, I avoid getting caught up in their turmoil. I want to avoid *catching* their mood, because I was that way once and I know how unhappy they are.

There was a time when I was so unclear about my limitations that I took on more than I could handle. I still tend to fall back into that pattern if I'm not careful. I was active in Al-Anon, going to school part-time, working, involved in half a dozen community affairs, and trying to be a perfect mother, wife and housekeeper all at once. There were constant conflicts and I always had to cut corners. As I neglected various jobs, guilt and feelings of inadequacy plagued me. I found myself out of breath even when I wasn't rushing, and irritable, with inappropriate reactions to small irritations. A glass of milk spilled on the freshly washed and waxed floor would send me into a rage because I just didn't have time to do it over, and appearances were so important, I thought.

How Important Is It helped me to reorganize my priorities and let go of the less important activities in order to be able

• • • • • • • • • •

to do justice to my really important responsibilities—to myself and to my family. *How Important Is It* helps me to say what I think without losing my self-control. I needn't win the point, or react to a nasty remark; stating my opinion is enough.

In a way, having lived with alcoholism gives us a fortunate perspective. Few things come close to being as devastating as trying to live with the problem without the help of Al-Anon. Everything else seems mild in comparison, and we can say *how important is it*, taking many things in our stride, confident in the knowledge that the really important things are being taken care of. The rest just doesn't matter all that much.

How Important Is It?

The other day I was scrubbing the floor on my hands and knees when my husband sneaked up behind me, in a loving mood. Before Al-Anon, I would have made a negative remark and just kept on scrubbing. But with the awareness I have gained in the program, I was able to realize that this was my husband, God's gift to me, the man I love dearly. That floor will be there for a long time. I knew my husband was more important than the floor, so we spent a beautiful afternoon together. I am so grateful for this program.

My Burning-House Decision

Many years ago, late at night I escaped from a burning house. When I was at the front door, I tried to go back up the flaming stairs to save a pretty box of writing paper. But I was stopped. I was unharmed—not because I did anything right but because I was lucky.

Once on the outside looking in, I was appalled at the risk I'd nearly taken just to try to save the pretty box of writing paper. Even more irrational, I had overlooked an easier and

● ● ● ● ● ● ● ● ● ●

safer way out. It was the crazy kind of thing people are apt to do in panic. I call it my burning-house decision.

I still live in a burning house, though the problem is not fire, but alcohol. Some time ago, before I came to Al-Anon, I was planning once again to run to what I thought was the nearest exit. It

meant driving through a snow-storm with four tired and fright-ened children, and maybe, or maybe not, reaching a summer cot-tage several miles away. But I was stopped. I called a number I'd been given through Al-Anon and a complete stranger said to me, "There is no need to run, there is no need to be fearful."

"I have to," I said. "He'll be home soon, he's been drinking and he will drink some more when he gets here."

"He'll drink anyway," she answered, "no matter what you do. He'll drink because his toast was burned this morning or because the sun isn't shining. It's late at night and if I were you I would just go to bed. Don't run and don't be fearful."

We were quite a sight, the five of us. The four crying children asking their frightened mother, "What did the woman tell us to do?"

"Why it's simple," I told them. "She said for us to go quietly to bed and to rest and not be afraid to walk and not to run, because if we run we will take the wrong way, and if we panic we may not find the exit at all."

● ● ● ● ● ● ● ● ● ●

Thanks to Al-Anon, I am once more standing outside the burning house and looking in. I see again the utter folly of trying to save the pretty box of writing paper, of driving late at night over a dangerous, snow-covered freeway. I suppose, as the resentful and self-pitying wife and mother, I had shock treatment in mind. But shock treatment for whom? For someone whose senses were too dulled by alcohol to respond? For myself, the hysterical mother, already in a state of shock? More than likely, we would have been highway statistics in the morning. And not because daddy drinks, but because mother panicked.

With Al-Anon I am learning to live with my burning house, to be on the outside looking in, to walk and not to run. I am learning to keep my sanity, to let go of the pretty box of writing paper. Best of all, I am learning not to make any more burning-house decisions.

Good Question

*L*ong ago someone asked me, "What's the worst thing that can happen to you?" My immediate answer then was, "I could lose my house!" As I examined that thought, I realized that I was losing my sanity worrying about a house. After much thought, I came to see that nothing and no one is worth my sanity. Thinking about what I believed to be the worst thing that could happen to me helped me to reorganize my sense of values and change my priorities.

● ● ● ● ● ● ● ● ● ●

JUST FOR TODAY

Just For Today

This day belongs to me. I will make every hour and minute better in the way I act and think.

I will breathe deeply every moment, living in the now. I will meditate, emptying my mind of all thought. This relaxes the body and mind and permits more profound ideas to enter. I will dwell on the idea that *heaven begins on earth.*

Today is a new page. I will take advantage of my open mind to do some reading. This day is a gift. I will live it joyously, fully. Today I understand that true love makes us forget ourselves in order to reach out to others. More and more freedom exists in my heart. I know that the light shines. I've seen it light up the eyes of members. I have been given the gift of speech. I haven't the right to keep quiet because of complacency, negligence or fear. I have something to say—short, perhaps, but full of life.

LET GO AND LET GOD

Surrender

I guess I hit bottom when I started thinking about doing away with my husband without getting caught. I certainly didn't think he was worth going to prison for. But my inner soul mustn't have been totally destroyed because my childhood teachings kept haunting me: *Thou shalt not kill.* I prayed and asked God to show me a way out of this torment.

The first thing I did was to go see an alcoholism counselor.

● ● ● ● ● ● ● ● ● ●

I sure didn't like him. Of course, I went to find out how to make my husband stop drinking. The counselor told me he couldn't help me; that there was no way anyone could make my husband stop drinking. I was mad and said, "What are you here for then?" From the tone of his voice he was mad, too. He said, "Look, lady, I'm here to counsel, not to make anybody do anything." So I said, "Thanks for nothing," and left.

After that, I decided that if my husband was going to drink, let him drink. But he wasn't going to drag me down with him. I didn't like the way we were living and refused to live that way any longer. I began to look to my Higher Power for guidance.

Instead of sitting at home waiting for trouble, I got out and got active. I stopped fighting with my husband when he came home late, drunk, and I did things I wanted to do, whether he wanted to or not.

He didn't like not being in the driver's seat any more; he drank even more and yelled at me every night. I prayed for more guidance, not to help my husband, just to help me. Then I remembered hearing about Al-Anon and got in touch with a group.

Now God is guiding me through the people in Al-Anon. I have learned to ask for help. I don't know what the future will bring. But I do believe if I keep my hands off and let God do it His way, He will give me the strength to face whatever comes.

● ● ● ● ● ● ● ● ● ●

Discussion Of Let Go And Let God

I had such a hard time understanding the meaning of detachment. I misinterpreted the word and became indifferent, incapable of real love. Because I didn't love myself, I had substituted a need to dominate. Now I prided myself on my coolness and lack of emotion during my husband's drinking episodes, not realizing that my apparent detachment was really a lack of feeling and caring.

Eventually, as reality became less painful, I could afford to feel again. My feelings for my husband came back, and I found myself getting upset. Obviously, I had not learned the right way to detach.

In order to let go of my husband, I had to believe that my Higher Power had our best interests at heart. When I became convinced that, no matter what happened, it was for the best, it was easy to let go.

I became able to make decisions without worrying about their effect on my husband's drinking. What freedom to be able to plan a picnic, or a visit with my brother, or an evening out with friends without worrying if my husband would resent it and drink! I always invited him along on family outings, but went without him if he was drinking, or not home when it was time to leave. I stopped worrying about how angry he would be when he learned we'd gone without him. The same thing applied if he began to drink while we were out—I'd leave with the children when I wanted to go home, always prepared ahead of time with an alternate method of transportation. No more waiting for him to finish his drinking, no more arguments as to who was to drive, no more pleading with him to not drink so much. His drinking became only his problem, when I arranged to have my plans go on as

• • • • • • • • • •

usual. Much less disruption of our family life took place, and I felt much better.

Letting go meant accepting what I couldn't change as God's will for me—for the time being. I believed there was a reason for it that made sense, even if I couldn't understand it just then. Looking back, I could see that things I'd viewed as rotten luck had turned out to be just what I needed at the time. And I trusted that the same thing was true of the present.

Letting go meant doing everything I could to change what needed change, but leaving the results to my Higher Power. When I made a decision to take a stand on violence—even to following through in the courts—I didn't know if my husband would stop drinking, get more violent, or walk right out. I was afraid of the possible consequences, and yet I believed that, no matter what happened, it would be for the best. I was confident my Higher Power would provide the strength to see me through. I didn't worry about the outcome, but concerned myself only with my part—doing my best.

Letting God take care of the results gave me so much freedom! I was free to do what I felt was right, without any guarantees that my actions would produce the desired effect. My concern was that my welfare, my growth and my dignity would be given a push in the right direction.

Letting go of the responsibility for my husband's drinking, and letting go of the consequences of decisions I felt were right, left me free to care about my husband as a person. I began to respect his right to be himself; to want him to get well for his sake, not just mine; to have compassion for his suffering, instead of resenting the pain I'd allowed him to inflict on me.

As I let go of the things over which I had no control and began to improve myself, my ability to love grew, too. I found I was able to love my husband in a healthy way, doing what was good for him, not necessarily what he wanted me to do.

● ● ● ● ● ● ● ● ● ●

I became able to see that it was important for him to face the consequences of his drinking. I learned that pain suffered as a result of drinking was a strong motivator towards sobriety; that gave me courage to keep my hands off drink-induced crises.

Although it wasn't pleasant to watch him suffer, I refused to give in because I knew I'd at last learned how to love him in a responsible way.

A Bird In The Bush

I was sitting alone in the house, engulfed in despair and en-joying it, when I came across a *FORUM* letter that seemed to apply to me. A girl from Texas had written how she would re-

tire to the backyard and listen to the birds sing when she felt down. How trite, I thought—help from the birds!

A short time later, I was on one of my long-distance, mind-purging solitary walks when I no-ticed that I was coming upon a bird singing merrily along in a bush. What the heck, I thought—give it a try. But as I passed the bush, he stopped singing—darned bird!

After another mile or so, I thought of another *FORUM* reader who said she had to speak to her Higher Power out loud for her to benefit from the contact. Glancing over my shoulder, I said out loud, "I can't hack it, God. Take this problem off my back." There was no roll of thunder or flash of lightning but, when I returned from the walk, the tremendous physical and mental strain had been miraculously removed. For the first

• • • • • • • • • •

time, I had really been able to *Let Go and Let God*. Help is where you find it, and it doesn't hurt to look for it in *The FO-RUM*.

Letting Go Again

The first thing I learned in Al-Anon was *Let Go and Let God*. That helped me to cope with the alcoholic's drinking. Now that he is sober in AA, I find my self resenting the long hours he spends with AA people.

I must let go again and remember that he didn't get sick overnight. His recovery may take years. I can find many things to occupy my time and, if I live one day at a time, all my days can be as beautiful as I want them to be.

LET IT BEGIN WITH ME

Continuous Effort Smooths Road To Health

After my husband came into AA I felt he should make up to our youngest child for the things he'd missed. I suggested, arranged and manipulated, with little success. Our home was often tense. This child became the recipient of verbal attacks and abuse.

Finally, I threw in the towel, realizing that there are children who have no fathers, or ones who are shiftless or actively drinking. At least my child had a sober father who worked and was a solid citizen. I decided to be the best mother I could be and let his dad play his role as he saw it. After I backed off, their relationship improved considerably.

Another of our problems was lack of communication. My husband would spend endless hours in deep discussions with

● ● ● ● ● ● ● ● ● ●

AA's but would throw roadblocks into my attempts to discuss anything more serious than what color to paint the kitchen.

The few times we had talked had helped to clear the air. Even if we'd come to an impasse and hadn't been able to solve a problem, we had been able to see each other's point of view. But his usual refusal to talk over problems was creating a lot of tension.

Actually, I was almost as reluctant as he to bring up unpleasant or painful issues. However, I believed it was vital to a healthy relationship. Applying the slogan *Let It Begin With Me*, I decided to speak my piece when the occasion arose. If an issue bothered me enough to make me sullen, irritable or cranky, I reasoned that since things were not going to be good around here, I might as well get my feelings off my chest. It soon became apparent that no way was my husband going to allow me to sound off without presenting his side. The result of course was communication!

Probably most shattering for me was my husband's sponsorship of women in AA. He insisted there was nothing going on, and that my jealousy was my problem. Once again I was faced with a problem about which I could do nothing. In Al-Anon I'd learned not to punish or condemn, I knew I shouldn't neglect my duties because someone else didn't conform to my ideas. So I kept myself busy with Al-Anon, my job, and housekeeping. We participated in AA social activities. He continued to be the dutiful husband he'd always been. But we merely co-existed.

One day I read an article in which several husbands aired their grievances against their wives. In every case there was nothing major, but each one complained of being neglected in small ways. When I turned the searchlight on myself, I was horrified. Years of functioning on my own had established habits of indifference, such as giving him a sandwich and cup of coffee without joining him, failing to greet him when he

• • • • • • • • • •

came home from work, not looking in on him when he was working in the garage, never buying a gift or adding an extra goody to his lunch. Standoffish, brisk and cold were apt descriptions of me.

When I became aware of this, I did a complete turn-around, clobbering him with attention. However, I gradually fell back into my careless habits. Then once again, I went on a campaign of attentiveness. Eventually this inconsistency evened off into a healthier pattern of loving concern.

I wasn't trying to change him, only to be the best person I could be. I'm trying to be less self-centered and more concerned about others. I had just about become resigned to my husband's brusque treatment of me, when he started to be really nice to me. The road has been long and filled with detours. However, we seem to be having smooth going for increasingly long stretches.

LISTEN AND LEARN

How To Listen

*L*earning to listen is one of the most difficult things I have had to do in Al-Anon. This is not to imply I have accomplished it but I'm making progress. This is what I've discovered about this precious achievement—to listen understandingly is not passive but a very muscular activity and it involves three distinct, active steps:

1. Keep out of it. Keep yourself removed. Keep objective. Don't intrude physically, verbally, mentally. Shut up. Listen. This is difficult and not passive.

2. Don't plan what you are going to say while another is talking. Don't think you can interrupt if you are quick enough about it. Don't think about how to solve, how to admon-

● ● ● ● ● ● ● ● ● ● ●

ish, how to advise, how to solace. Don't think. Listen.

3. Understand what is being felt as well as what is being said. Hear every nuance of tone and meaning. Listen to intent as well as content.

If I am able to practice any one or all of the above, any meeting becomes the best I've ever attended. There is a time to share and a time just to listen.

LIVE AND LET LIVE

Discussion Of Live And Let Live

I was talking to someone the other day who was bemoaning the fact that his efforts to change have had so little effect on his children. He sees that patterns of behavior are passed on from generation to generation; that the children of alcoholics often become alcoholics themselves or marry alcoholics, no matter how much sobriety or change has taken place in the home. He concluded that people learn how to act and react very early in life, and that real changes, if any, take many many generations. He was filled with a sense of hopelessness as he went on to say that no matter how much he accomplished, no one would remember it a hundred years from now.

I don't agree with his thinking. I believe we can, by changing ourselves, stop the vicious cycle of emotional illness from being passed on. We may not achieve it all at once, and our children certainly do have scars. But we can send them into the world armed with the tools of the program, the wisdom we have gained, and our good example. We can, by living our lives to the fullest, better prepare them to live theirs. We can, by facing our problems squarely and bravely, teach them not to be afraid of theirs. After that, we have to let go and let them live, make their choices, make their mistakes.

● ● ● ● ● ● ● ● ● ●

It isn't easy to let others live their lives as they choose. I tried desperately to live my husband's life for him. Making him happy and finding the solution to his drinking problem were my primary goals. I made a real crusade of it—and failed. Once in Al-Anon, I learned to allow him the right to make his own choices, to live his life as he wished to live it. I learned I didn't have the right to force my values on another.

But old habits die hard. Every so often, when working with a resistant newcomer, I want to shake her and say, "Can't you see what you're doing? Why don't you... ." But I usually catch myself and realize that only the person who is going to live with the consequences of a decision has the right to make that decision. Not I. I have to let live and help others by living my life in such a way that they will be tempted to try to do the same.

Perhaps the most difficult for many of us is letting go of our children. So many feelings are tied up in what our children do and how they turn out. We want them to be happy, of course, but also feel they're a reflection on us. After all, *the apple doesn't fall far from the tree.* Depending on our sense of values, we may get very upset if our children choose a different lifestyle from ours, or reject the things we think are important. We may decide we know what's best for them; or, wanting to protect them from pain, insist they profit from our experience. We may forget that experience is the best teacher— our own, not somebody else's—and that children learn by making mistakes.

It's no easy task to develop the emotional detachment that allows us to let those we love suffer growing pains. But it's easier, I think, if we concentrate on making our own lives meaningful.

After I learned that I could no longer make my husband's sobriety my central goal, I felt quite a large void in my life. Eventually, I replaced it with trying to fulfill myself as a per-

● ● ● ● ● ● ● ● ● ● ●

son, to develop my potential, and to help others. It is true—no one will remember me a hundred years from now, either. I'll never be rich or famous. But I believe my efforts are like pebbles tossed in a pond. The things that form and move away from that pebble are silent, but they continue to move out further and further, and have far-reaching effects. If I can help someone in Al-Anon, and that person in turn helps someone else, and so on, my efforts will not be wasted. This is what gives my life meaning and purpose.

From Ann Landers' Column

Dear Ann:

It is Sunday afternoon, our 13 year-old boy went to a ball game, the 10 and 12 year-old girls are in the neighbor's swimming pool, and my husband went to his favorite tavern to get drunk. I'm not writing for advice.

A few years ago I would have been crying my eyes out, or venting my anger to a friend on the telephone. But today I am calm, content, and very happy with life. Why? Because I listened to you and joined Al-Anon.

Every woman who is married to an alcoholic must at some point decide whether she is going to allow his problem to defeat her or learn how to live with it. Since I joined Al-Anon I love and understand my husband more than ever. Our marriage is better than most marriages where no drinking problem exists. Due to my changed attitude toward my husband, he has become a better father and a better person.

At the moment my husband has expressed no interest in joining AA. I hope one day he will do so, but he must come to the decision himself. If he never comes to it, it's all right with me. I have learned to live with him, and I appreciate the many other wonderful blessings in my life.

● ● ● ● ● ● ● ● ● ●

Please, Ann, keep telling people about Al-Anon. It's a life-saver—both literally and figuratively.

One Day At A Time

Thrill Of Accomplishment

As a result of daily reading of *One Day At A Time In Al-Anon,* thinking about the slogans, measuring my actions and decisions against the standards of the Serenity Prayer, accepting guidance from my Higher Power (and not just after disasters), I have recently experienced the thrill of accomplishment. I have come out of the despair which came about through unemployment and separation. I now am employed and staying that way and bringing joy to my family. I have gained the courage to become the person I was intended to be, joyfully, one day at a time. As someone once said, "Today, well-lived, makes every yesterday a dream of happiness and every tomorrow a vision of hope."

A Positive Approach

I enjoy each day as it comes. Living one day at a time keeps things in perspective. Counting my blessings helps keep me happy. I don't keep an unpleasant thought in my mind any longer than necessary. If it's a problem that needs attention, I pray about it. This calms me. Then I face facts and decide as soon as possible what to do; I carefully prepare, and do it. When I have done what I think is best, I don't worry about the reactions of others. The results are up to my Higher Power.

• • • • • • • • • •

SERENITY PRAYER

Serenity Prayer

G*od grant me the serenity to accept the things I cannot change.*

We mustn't confuse God with our childhood image of daddy—we must believe in His power and ask for serenity with humility. It will come when we surrender our lives to Him.

From this oasis of quietness, we can accept the burdens of the things we cannot change. They become light when we realize we are never given anything beyond our strength.

Courage to change the things I can.

Courage is said to be fears that have said their prayers. Having said our prayers, we ask for and receive what is our unquestionable right: dignity, self-respect, happiness. The path is easier when we stop groveling and whining, begging for crumbs from the *why me* table.

We can change ourselves from weak-kneed shadows to strong and tolerant persons once we've accepted what can't be changed.

And wisdom to know the difference.

When we accept our burden, we receive courage. The difference is so clear, we wonder why the darkness was so dense.

Stick-To-It-Iveness

My worst shortcoming has been lack of persistence. If I didn't achieve my goals right away, I just threw up my hands and said *oh, what's the use?* I found it far too easy to simply accept things as they were after my attempts to change had failed. I found that I really did not want the wisdom to know the difference because that might require courage on my part.

To acquire patience and persistence, I have developed my own version of the Serenity Prayer; God grant me the serenity to accept for now the things I cannot change, and when I have acquired the wisdom, then help me to have the courage to follow through with the changing process.

Recovering From Hurt

Several weeks ago I was deeply hurt by something someone said to me. *How could they hurt me after all I've done for them?* I asked myself. My first reaction was to hurt back.

After a bout of tears, carrying-on and self-pity, I thought of the Serenity Prayer. Suddenly, I realized that no attempt on my part to change this person was going to work. I have to accept others as they are. Serenity comes only when I can do this. When I try to force a change, I only upset myself.

What has worked for me is finding the courage to change myself and my attitudes, and discovering that I actually do like myself and am not really bad; that there are people who accept me as I am; that there's no need to put on an act to impress people or win friends.

With my change in attitude, I find I'm getting a different response from people. As long as I accept myself, other people no longer seem to be a threat to my serenity. The world

● ● ● ● ● ● ● ● ● ●

gives back what I give it.

I now know that those who hurt others are to be pitied. They must be terribly unhappy themselves to lash out that way. I mustn't take their behavior personally. They are also God's children. There is much room for improvement in my life, but it can come only from changes in my own attitudes and behavior. I now know the joy of beginning each day expectantly, confident that it will hold good things for me.

• • • • • • • • • •

• • • • • • • • • •

The Steps

Within the Twelve Steps, I find the foundation
to a life of love.

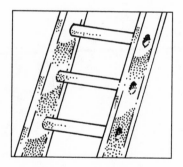

• • • • • • • • • •

THE STEPS IN GENERAL

Program Of Love

Within the Twelve Steps, I find the foundation to a life of love:

1. *We admitted we were powerless over alcohol—that our lives had become unmanageable.*

In this Step, love is *humility*. With this admission that we are human, we become open to God's love. It is the doorway to a new life.

2. *Came to believe that a Power greater than ourselves could restore us to sanity.*

In this Step, love is *faith*. We believe that in receiving love from our Higher Power, and in giving it, we will regain sanity.

3. *Made a decision to turn our will and our lives over to the care of God as we understood Him.*

In this Step, love is *surrender*. We give to God our wills and our lives, thereby entering into a loving relationship with Him.

4. *Made a searching and fearless moral inventory of ourselves.*

In this Step, love is *honesty*. We look at our lives, at our failures to love and be loved, at the ways we have loved. Honesty opens us to more love.

5. *Admitted to God, to ourselves and to another human being the exact nature of our wrongs.*

In this Step, love is *responsibility*. When we admit failure to

• • • • • • • • • •

love and be loved, we accept responsibility for our wrongs. We receive God's forgiveness, His love. When we open ourselves to others, we are performing an act of love.

6. *Were entirely ready to have God remove all these defects of character.*

In this Step, love is *trust.* We trust that God's love will be present in our lives.

7. *Humbly asked Him to remove our shortcomings.*

In this Step, love is *action.* Asking God to help us is an act of love.

8. *Made a list of all persons we had harmed and became willing to make amends to them all.*

In this Step, love is *brotherhood.* Just as we need a loving relationship with God, we also need one with our brothers.

9. *Made direct amends to such people wherever possible, except when to do so would injure them or others.*

In this Step, love is *outgoing.* We attempt to restore a loving relationship with those we have harmed.

10. *Continued to take personal inventory and when we were wrong, promptly admitted it.*

In this Step, love is *continuous.* We strive to maintain our love of God and our fellow man by being aware of anything that might interfere with it.

11. *Sought through prayer and meditation to improve our conscious contact with God as we understood Him, praying only for knowledge of His will for us and the power to carry that out.*

In this Step, love is *living.* We turn to God for direction, seeking His will in all we do.

12. *Having had a spiritual awakening as a result of these*

● ● ● ● ● ● ● ● ● ●

Steps, we tried to carry this message to others, and to practice these principles in all our affairs,

In this Step, love is *gratitude.* Having received God's love, we give it to our neighbors in gratitude. Love is giving.

POWERLESSNESS

W*e admitted we were powerless over alcohol—that our lives had become unmanageable.*

Teenage Alcoholism

Living with a recovering teenage alcoholic is both frustrating and rewarding. We had no idea that our fifteen year-old son had a drinking problem, but we did know something was wrong. His behavior was completely unpredictable, and his school grades went from all A's to D's and F's. We never knew if he would go to school, or how long he would stay before being suspended. All our lives became completely unmanageable.

My husband and I were both convinced that our son's problems were our fault. Thanks to Al-Anon, we gradually began to believe that we were not at fault, and that we were powerless to keep him from drinking.

He was sober four months before he had a slip, and it has now been five months. Our main problem is trying to distinguish between alcoholic behavior and typical teenage behavior. We are relying on regular attendance at meetings, and reading of AA and Al-Anon literature to help us come through this successfully.

● ● ● ● ● ● ● ● ● ●

Something Lost, Something Gained

I was running my life, my job, my husband's life, his job, my father's life, his job, and just about everyone's life. If only I'd had the insight then to see that my attitude was only building resentments. I didn't realize the dangerous game I was playing, feeding my husband's illness, literally killing him with kindness. All my schemes to keep him from drinking fell apart.

I gradually came to realize that, while I'm powerless over others, I'm not powerless over myself. I held on to the love, patience and understanding of my group while my old ideas fell apart. What I thought was a weakness, a powerlessness, turned into an inner strength I'd never known before.

Although I've given up so many things to my Higher Power, I've gained so much more—peace of mind, serenity, emotional growth, self-confidence. But I don't think I'll ever be grownup enough to be able to handle anyone else's life again.

Takes First Step

I felt instant resistance to the first part of Step One, probably because my life was coasting along on its miserable merry-go-round and any change meant too much effort. Why is it so difficult to admit powerlessness? Perhaps because we think we must admit we are powerless over everything. But the Step says only 'powerless over alcohol.' We have power over ourselves; we can change.

Those twelve words in the First Step sound so easy, but I found them very hard until I realized that the surrender of power meant letting the other person go. Suddenly I realized I was free. My teeth unclenched, my muscles relaxed, my morale began to build up as I took things one day at a time. If we want power, we can use it to guide ourselves. If we want to be managers, we can manage ourselves.

• • • • • • • • • •

FAITH

Came to believe that a Power greater than ourselves could restore us to sanity.

Step Two

I came to Al-Anon as an atheist and stayed in that lonely and depressed state for a very long time. Slowly, I turned to another power—the group, God, goodness, or whatever. The name is not important.

My words and actions were insane. I was in an almost constant state of anxiety and fear. I spent many sleepless nights over imagined plights. By three or four in the morning I had almost convinced myself that if these things hadn't happened by dawn, they most certainly would have before the week was out.

Tired and haggard, I faced the new day with little hope and a chronic case of *what did I ever do to deserve this?* I wished I had never been born.

I had uncontrollable rages, temper fits with the children. I took personal offense at everything, including the way the soap opera plot was going.

Then my husband joined AA. After a brief period of happiness, I found I was still unhappy. I returned to Al-Anon, doggedly still an atheist.

My group could have turned me off very easily with religion or intolerance for my lack of belief. But they let me grow, slowly. When they had something that good, it must have been a struggle for them not to push it on me, ever so gently.

● ● ● ● ● ● ● ● ● ●

Slowly came the belief, and with it, the relief. In so many ways, this Power has shown me a better way. One day at a time I am getting stronger, saner and calmer. It's frightening to discover that the more I learn, the greater that horizon becomes. But I now know that with the help of my Higher Power I can bring order and serenity into my life.

Al-Anon didn't preach to me or dictate what I must believe; it allowed me to open my mind and think things out for myself.

The Second Step

*T*his Step means believing your Higher Power can and will help you. It isn't easy. Until you experience that Power and learn to trust it, you can be quite uncomfortable with the idea.

You can't quite grasp this business of a Higher Power helping you? Just try it. What have you got to lose? He can hardly do worse than you, can He? Doesn't letting your Higher Power run your life make more sense than letting somebody else's illness run it? That's what's been going on!

Even at its worst, what does the word *insane* make you think of? Losing touch with reality? Well, what else is living in the past, cherishing resentments, distorting memories, fearing a future that isn't even real yet? What else is panic, and thoughts of suicide?

Do you think of the man who imagines he's Napoleon? Well, haven't you tried to be the emperor who ran things, who dictated what was good and bad for others? Do you think of the man who imagines he's a light bulb or a sandwich? Haven't you let others treat you as though you weren't human?

Do you think of the man who imagines he's God? What else is it when you sit in judgment of others?

● ● ● ● ● ● ● ● ● ● ●

When we think of what's been going on, the word *insane* is not too much. I find that cold splash of a word helps me to realize just where I was, and where I'd be without Al-Anon.

Overcoming Fear With Faith

*I'*ve often spoken of the fears that ruled my life: fear of rejection and fear of failure. There were others too: fear of pain, fear of loneliness, fear of ridicule and pity, fear of embarrassment, fear of anger—my own and others', fear of honesty, fear of confrontation, and finally, fear of people, of the telephone, of the future, of life itself.

Looking back, I am sometimes amazed that I functioned as well as I did, and that I was able to live with that level of discomfort for so long. And I'm equally amazed to think that a program for living devised by two men in the throes of alcoholism could have wrought such a change in me!

Faith is absolutely essential to my physical and mental well-being. First, there is faith in my Higher Power, that force for good upon which I rely to bring about the best from my best efforts. My belief in this Higher Power helps me to listen with an open mind, to dare to try things I'd never tried before. The knowledge that the future will be what it will be, and that I don't have to be responsible for how things turn out, only for what I do, is a great source of comfort. By believing in my Higher Power, I no longer have to fear failure or the future.

Next, I must have faith in people. I would go insane if I didn't have people in my life who accept and love me as I am, who hear me, who respond to my needs. I believe that people are basically good, that they can get better, that love can bring out the best in others. When I believe in others and love them, I no longer need to fear them or fear being honest with them. I can confront problems, express my feelings, and let

• • • • • • • • • •

others express theirs.

Last, my faith in myself, my sense of adequacy, is inseparable from my feelings of self-worth. I have felt tremendous pain, both physical and psychological, and I have survived. I have come to the point where I realize that I must do many things alone. I am, in the final analysis, responsible for myself.

Because I believe in myself, in my ability to cope, in my ability to ask for help, to change, to get better, I no longer fear ridicule, pity or embarrassment. It's okay to make mistakes. Those who need to ridicule or pity me are responding to their own inner discomfort. Their ridicule does not make me ridiculous, nor does their pity make me pathetic. I am what I am in spite of what others may see. I know that if someone rejects me, it doesn't mean I'm unlovable, only that they aren't loving.

It is wonderful to welcome life with a smile. That's not to say I have no problems or concerns. I have deep concerns for my children. And there are many challenges in my life which give me pause: new jobs, new responsibilities, new relationships. But it's great to be able to tackle all of these knowing that, even if I should fall flat on my face, there's still tomorrow. I can try again. So can you.

TRUST

Made a discussion to turn our will and our lives over to the care of God as we understood Him.

Prayer Is Pivotal Force

I wrote this when I was at the end of my rope. Since then I have been led to serenity by my Higher Power.

• • • • • • • • • •

Dear God, take my life and let me live serenely for today. Open my mind to happy thoughts. Take away my self-pity, I don't want it. Take away ill-will toward others. Make it possible for me to feel joy, love, compassion. Help me to accept what is, to hold my tongue, to do my daily tasks, to let go with love.

Take away my worry about the future. Make me realize that in Your hands everything will be provided for, that I have no control over anything but myself, that today is precious and will soon be gone.

Help me to remember that all the hatred and pain that are directed at me are the hatred and pain the other person is feeling toward himself.

Thank you for your willingness to accept my burdens and lighten my load.

Fear Or Faith

Fear knocked. Faith answered. No one was there.

That saying is a source of strength for me. Fear ran my life—fear of the unknown, of being rejected, hurt, ridiculed, fear of nameless worries, and most of all the *what ifs*. I turned from a sensible girl to a quivering mass of nothing, incapable of making decisions.

Fear knocked with questions like: What if he doesn't come home? What if he drinks? What if she smokes pot, takes drugs? What if they sneak around? What if she wrecks the car? What if he drinks and he's supposed to be watching the children?

Some of these questions were legitimate. Somewhere I read that fear is nothing more or less than a distorted faith in the negative things of life and the evils that might happen to us. I began to realize that most of my fears came from dwelling

● ● ● ● ● ● ● ● ● ●

on negative things. I then read in *One Day At A Time In Al-Anon,* "Granted these things can happen, but when they don't we have put ourselves through needless suffering and made ourselves even less prepared to deal with them if they should come."

Finally light bulbs turned on. These questions came to my mind: Who am I hurting? Myself. Am I enjoying it? No. What can I do about it? Things I was learning from the meetings began to make sense.

So I had to put what I had learned into practice. Just for today, I will not project. I'll bring my life into this one day and will think positive rather than negative thoughts. I will deal with things as they come, and not waste my time worrying about stuff that may not happen. I will quit punishing myself.

Faith answered. If I have enough faith, fear will go away. Where do I get the strength? The Third Step. More light bulbs in my head. If I was to believe, there would be risks to take. Risks like letting him handle the money, allowing him to live his life as he sees fit, asking a beloved child to move out of the house. And after each risk my feeling inside was so much better. Then there was more belief in my Higher Power and less fear in me.

No one was there. Fear leaves me when I rely on my Higher Power, try to live one day at a time and don't project into the future. I don't succeed all the time but for the major part of each day I do. Fear is controlled so long as I keep a conscious contact with God.

● ● ● ● ● ● ● ● ● ●

Verbal And Nonverbal Communication

*I*n the book of Ecclesiastes it says, "For everything there is a season, and a time for every matter under Heaven . . . a time to keep silence, and a time to speak. . . ." From this I have concluded that there is no single answer to communication with an alcoholic. My life with active drinkers, first my parents, then my husband, was a lot like *walking on eggs*. It was living in an unhealthy kind of silence punctuated by bursts of violent anger and accusation, an unhealthy kind of speech. In Al-Anon I learned that either approach is a dead end; that for my own health, my silence must be serene, and my speech detached but loving. For we speak with more than our voices; just by attending Al-Anon meetings I was telling my husband there was a severe problem in our home and that I was willing to recover.

The fearful silence I'd kept while *walking on eggs* had told him so many things I didn't mean: that I hated him, that he was at fault, all the same things I shouted at him when I was angry. Silence can be more cruel than speech, for in our imagining we put into the other's mouth words more horrible than he or she would dream of uttering.

It is necessary for me to tell my husband how I feel, but only if I can do so with detachment and love. It is the beginning of communication, a communication that has grown and flowered with his sobriety and my growth in Al-Anon. There are times when silence is equally important, and silence has been the key to quelling one of my worst defects—anger. A prayerful silence has an unmistakable quality. It is calming and it produces serenity. When I practice Step Three with my whole heart, turning my will and life over to God, I will know when and how to speak or keep silent. For, indeed, there is a time for both.

● ● ● ● ● ● ● ● ● ●

No Man is Wise Enough By Himself

After I was in Al-Anon about two years, the pink cloud vanished and I found myself getting upset at meetings because it seemed to me that very few of my fellow members were sticking to the principles of Al-Anon. Too many were giving advice to newcomers and too many were leading the meetings astray by bringing in pronouncements from authority figures outside the program. There was much talk of alcoholism and alcoholics. I often came away from meetings less serene than when I arrived.

Since then I have realized I was reverting to the negativism I had brought with me into Al-Anon. Sure these negative things were happening, but I was picking out only the things I did not like and ignoring the positive elements that I needed for my own recovery.

I started to try to cultivate patience and tolerance in the realization that I am as powerless over other members of Al-Anon as I am over alcohol. It is not my duty nor within my ability to set other people right. The desire to do so is a major part of my illness. When it comes my turn to speak, I can share only my own experience, strength and hope and keep my own feet on the path that is best for me. Somehow when I do this I find I can trust others to do the same and the miracle of mutual assistance occurs again.

As I continue in Al-Anon I begin to see more and more often that there is a spiritual renewal at every meeting. I can respond to it or I can shut it out. When I insist on clinging to my own individuality and unique wisdom I am erecting the walls again.

Last week a friend in Al-Anon called to tell me he had discovered a little bit of what the Twelfth Tradition means when it states, "Anonymity is the spiritual foundation of all our Tra-

• • • • • • • • • •

ditions, ever reminding us to place principles above personalities."

He had just lost his wife through a lingering and pain-ridden illness that had also destroyed his financial security. He wanted to tell me that the concept of anonymity had helped him to accept his suffering. He realized he had not been singled out for special punishment. Terrible tragedy had come to him, but he found the help he needed when he humbly abandoned the idea of his own uniqueness. An ego trip was no more beneficial in times of trouble than in times of success.

I was able to respond to him because I had just recently arrived at a similar destination by my own understanding of the Third Step. Earlier in the year my daughter had called to tell me my youngest granddaughter had an enlarged head and might be suffering from hydrocephalus. For some reason this led me to look back at my life and realize for the first time, that my love could not protect the ones I loved.

My only sister had died in the first year of her marriage from blood poisoning that could be cured today but was fatal before antibiotics were discovered. My mother had died in a state hospital, victim of lead poisoning that had destroyed her sanity. My first marriage had ended in a divorce that separated me from my baby daughter, destroying a relationship I was never able to restore. My second wife, despite her intelligence, beauty and artistic talents, had discovered she was an alcoholic. My oldest son was the victim of an obscure and incurable disease which twisted his bones and made them fragile. Lately he had also begun to show signs of other meta-

● ● ● ● ● ● ● ● ● ●

bolic developments that posed new threats.

How many reminders did I need before I came to realize that my will was not governing my life and deciding the fate of those I love. I *made a decision to turn my will and my life over to the care of God as I understood Him.* I know this does not mean that somehow my decision will restore my powers and all my troubles will vanish. It means that I am to turn my life over to the reality of existence and to stop insisting on setting up dreams of what reality should be.

We *practice these principles in all our affairs.* It is a strange paradox that when I can give up my own concept of my unique ability and suffering, I do become a more complete human being. When I acknowledge that my existence includes darkness, sickness and death, I am able to appreciate the sunlight, what health is and what it means to be alive.

SELF-EXAMINATION

Made a searching and fearless moral inventory of ourselves.

Mother Admits Making Mistakes Too

My greatest fault was that I was conscious of none. However, once I took an honest look at myself as the Fourth Step suggests, I found great comfort in acknowledging my faults to my Higher Power, myself and another human being. I am able to think more clearly now and enjoy listening to others with similar problems.

I overlooked my son's drinking and made excuses for it before he was married. When marriage and fatherhood didn't calm him down, I blamed his wife. After his marriage broke up, I compulsively rescued him and covered up for him. Whenever anyone mentioned the word alcoholic, I would strike out savagely. I became bitter and selfishly isolated myself from

• • • • • • • • • •

family and friends. I would have died rather than admit my son was an alcoholic.

However, as the drinking progressed, my cover-ups became monstrous. I lied to his employer, to family and neighbors. I got him out of every jam, cleaned his apartment, washed his clothes, even took food to him after dark and forced him to eat.

After a third car accident from which he walked away with only minor injuries, all the resentments and tensions I'd been bottling up exploded. I shouted and raged like a shrew and hit him with every bit of sarcasm I could muster. When he responded only with "Get off my back," I felt as if the last drop of blood had been drained from my body. What a terrible blow, after all I'd done for him!

Completely defeated, I contacted Al-Anon at my daughter's suggestion. In eight short weeks I have come face to face with myself and the damage I had been doing. I have stayed off my son's back and he is now active in AA where I hope he will find a new life. I have the firm foundation for my recovery in Al-Anon.

PERSONAL RE-EXAMINATION

Continued to take personal inventory and when we were wrong promptly admitted it.

Al-Anon's Encouragement

Taking inventory at regular intervals is one of our principal Steps and a great source of personal encouragement. Frequent balancing of personal debits and credits shows how we're doing—how we're progressing. Just like retail merchants, we have to keep our books balanced to see where we're heading.

● ● ● ● ● ● ● ● ● ●

There's another kind of inventory, to give us additional encouragement, which also comes right out of the merchant's handbook. It's called *comparison shopping*—seeing what he's got; how his merchandise stacks up in price, quality and style with competitors.

Sometime when you want a big lift, or need encouragement in your Al-Anon work, just do a bit of *comparison shopping* with, say, a new member or maybe the last person you Twelfth-Stepped or sponsored. See what he has and compare it with what you have in the way of serenity, peace of mind and the sure knowledge that Al-Anon truly is the way of life for steady spiritual growth. Then sharing the richness which Al-Anon brings to each one who vigilantly practices it, bring encouragement beyond and above the effort involved.

Progress Report Tells It Like It Is

*U*nder our new trimester system in our public schools, we now send home a progress report on each child every six weeks. We give his average to date but also mark certain characteristics as Excellent, Good, Fair or Poor, on attributes like, *Cooperates with teachers and classmates,* and *Makes up work after absences.* There must be a dozen to mark.

It set me thinking about such reports. Our literature speaks of *progress, not perfection,* and I doodled a kind of progress report for me. It was not for self-condemnation or self-judgment but a kind of stock-taking. I have to back off and look at myself sometimes.

I worked out the following statements about how I work the Al-Anon program for my private review:

I am in this program to work on myself.

I am able to accept what I cannot change.

On the other hand, I do not accept abuse or unacceptable behavior.

● ● ● ● ● ● ● ● ● ●

I change the things I can (mostly myself).

I have released my loved ones, placing them in God's hands.

I place principles above personalities.

I am available when I am needed, whether by a group or a person.

I respect anonymity.

I give compassion but not sick sympathy.

I ask for help when I need it.

I have given up enjoying martyrdom.

I work the Steps.

I have a sponsor and use her/him.

I keep the Traditions and encourage my group to do so.

I talk when I am asked and can do so.

I never give direct advice.

I know that I am entirely responsible for my attitude and behavior.

I remember to express gratitude, not pride.

Avoiding Slips By Staying Mentally Sober

SYMPTOMS LEADING TO RELAPSE:

• **Exhaustion**—I mustn't allow myself to become overly tired, or keep myself so busy that home and children take second place. Good health and rest are important; when I feel well, I'm more apt to think well. When I feel badly, I say and do things I'm sure to be sorry for later.

• **Dishonesty**—This begins with covering up for the drinker.

• • • • • • • • • •

I won't make excuses to family, friends, the boss.

• **Impatience**—Things are not happening fast enough, or others are not doing what I think they should.

• **Argumentativeness**—Reacting to the alcoholic's accusations by arguing just gives him an excuse to drink.

• **Depression**—I must deal with it and talk about it; not allow it to continue.

• **Frustration**—Things are not going my way.

• **Self-pity**—*Why me? Nobody appreciates me.*

• **Threats**—I mustn't say things I don't mean.

• **Complacency**—I should continue to attend meetings although things are better for the time being. Prayer, meditation, daily inventory are all important.

• **Expecting Too Much**—It's a plus if others change for the better, but I won't let it be a problem if they don't. I can't expect others to change just because I have. I must set realistic goals, and do my best.

MEDITATION AND PRAYER

Sought through prayer and meditation to improve our conscious contact with God as we understood Him, praying only for knowledge of His will for us and the power to carry that out.

Eleventh Step

I sat alone after my family went to bed, trying to fathom how one can go about trying to bring his Higher Power into sharper focus. I think it happened to me tonight. I have a taste of that elusive serenity; I feel the beauty of the world that transcends the quest for things and power. I have life's necessities and many of its luxuries: a husband I love, children I cherish, excellent health, improving family relationships.

I am no longer slovenly about myself or my responsibilities. I accept what life brings me, going along with what keeps my husband content and sober. I don't have to retort when baited, and can't be insulted unless I allow myself to be.

I used to think I was last in everything; that my husband took the gravy and I got the crumbs. I pictured myself as the poor little martyred slave-wife who walked three steps obediently behind her master.

Today I walk beside my husband in support, not behind him in submission. It makes a difference! And that's what I talked to my Higher Power about tonight.

How Would I Like It?

When I need to be frank with my husband about something, I weigh my comments by asking: *How would I like it if he said that to me?* This has really made me watch my tongue. I seek guidance from my Higher Power. When in doubt, I keep my mouth shut. And I watch my timing a little better than I used to.

I believe anything can be said as long as it is not motivated by hatred or resentment, but by a true desire to reach a better understanding.

God's Will Revealed Through Al-Anon Program

Some people are born with such beautiful natures that they instinctively divine God's will. But ordinary human beings like me and many others, learn to know it or feel it only after they have wrestled with themselves through concentrating on the program and really working it. Even then it is difficult.

• • • • • • • • • •

There was a time when the answer for me seemed obvious: if two courses of action presented themselves in a difficult situation, I was sure the easy one to take was undoubtedly my own will and the hard one God's. Somewhat later I recognized this as the same sort of jaundiced judgment G.I.s had of army regulations: "There are two ways of doing things, the right way and the army way."

Gradually, helped by the Eleventh Step, I perceived an unwelcome tinge of self-pity in my idea that the hard way was God's. I also saw it was far from true. Because I had not wholly accepted alcoholism as an illness, I rebelled against it and persisted in beating my head against a wall. That surely was the difficult way and just as surely was not God's will.

It takes subhuman insensitivity to resist spiritual growth if one adopts Al-Anon's philosophy and seriously tries to live it. Thus I gradually progressed to the point where I could see that I was not a howling success at being *master of my fate . . . captain of my soul.*

Henley's poem had always offended me; I believe now it was because he seemed to brag so about "my head is bloody but unbowed." And when he came to "I am the master of my fate" and so on, I just felt he was whistling himself past a graveyard. I much prefer Carpenter's "For Hope may anchor, Faith may steer, but Love, great love is captain of the soul." That's the kind of captain I want to be.

As I slowly learned to control instinctive reactions to disagreeable situations, I became more conscious of how I should live. The voice of conscience was never a *still small* one to me. It was more a nagging feeling that I should do better, be a bigger person, more tolerant and should make myself rise above selfish considerations.

So I did grow spiritually—some, at least. I gave myself a chance to consider what God would think I ought to do. I asked His help in guiding me to the best way to live and to

• • • • • • • • • •

show me how to do everything in His name—not for personal gratification, glory nor to impress anyone else. I knew that if I could accomplish that end, I'd be sure I was following His will. So, I just keep trying, every day.

How To Know God's Will

The problem for me lies in trying to tell the difference between God's will and mine. If I have sought through prayer and meditation God's will on a specific problem, then I seem to have an inkling of what is right and reasonable. I begin to act on that nudge, at the same time continuing to pray. I firmly believe that once I have turned the matter over to my Higher Power, if what I am doing is not His will, the direction will be changed.

The more I am able to run my life this way, the more trusting I become. The result is not guaranteed to please me, but then I can't see the end of the road. The will of God may seem hard at times but good is always served.

The way that seems right to me is not necessarily the best for me spiritually. I certainly would not have chosen the pain and frustration of an alcoholic marriage, but what a beautiful life we have now because of AA and Al-Anon! When life is not so beautiful, we have the tools to work it out.

To determine whether or not I am using good judgment, I ask myself:

1. Is my thinking clear?
2. Will my decision bring me peace?
3. Am I treating all concerned with love? (Sometimes this means *tough* love.)
4. Can good come from my decision?
5. Have I really let go of my will in the matter?

If the answers are yes, then I know I'm on the right track.

• • • • • • • • • •

• • • • • • • • • •

The Traditions

*I*f the Traditions can hold together such a diverse group of individuals as those found in Al-Anon, they can surely be used as a springboard for families recovering from severe stress, in dire need of a simple frame of reference, and a sense of direction.

• • • • • • • • • •

THE TRADITIONS IN GENERAL

My Family's Traditions

If the Traditions can hold together such a diverse group of individuals as those found in Al-Anon, they can surely be used as a springboard for families recovering from severe stress, in dire need of a simple frame of reference, and a sense of direction. Mine was such a family, and this translation has helped me over many a hump in the years of recovery.

1. Our common welfare should come first; personal progress for the greatest number depends upon unity.

2. For our family purpose there is but one authority, a loving God as He may express Himself in our family conscience. Parents and elders are but trusted servants. They lead by example.

3. Relatives, when gathered together for mutual support and participation may call themselves a family. The only requirement for membership is that there be a common bond of mutuality.

4. Our family should be self-governing except in matters affecting relatives or mankind as a whole.

5. Our family has but one purpose—to be mutually supportive of one another. We do this by practicing the Twelve Steps ourselves, by encouraging and understanding each other and by welcoming and giving comfort to families with like concerns.

6. Our family ought never become so involved with outside issues as to let problems of money, property or prestige divert us from our primary spiritual aim. Although a separate entity, we should always cooperate with our relatives and neighbors.

• • • • • • • • • •

7. Our family should be fully self-supporting, declining outside contributions.

8. Education to our way of life should be person to person but our service centers (school, church, AA and Al-Anon) may employ special workers.

9. Our family, as such, ought to be democratic. We may elect public officials to represent us.

10. Our family has no opinion or judgment of other ways of life. We live and let live.

11. Our way of life is based on attraction by example. We do not use our family or anyone else for personal recognition or gain. We need to guard with special care the privacy and personal rights of all persons.

12. Humility is the spiritual foundation of all our Traditions, ever reminding us to place principles above personalities.

A Short Version Of The Twelve Traditions

I   All for one—one for all.

II   We have but one boss—a loving God.

III   Relatives of alcoholics help others to help themselves.

IV   We run our own affairs—that is enough for most of us.

V   We have but one purpose—that's a full-time job.

VI   We tend to our own business.

VII   We pay our own way.

VIII   We hire people to do things we cannot do.

IX   We don't organize but we make some arrangements.

X   We stay out of squabbles—we might fight dirty.

• • • • • • • • • •

XI   We let people know we exist—politely and in good taste.

XII Anonymity is our cloak of protection; it protects us—it does not hide us.

Best Medicine For What Ails Your Group

Recently, I began to see things happening in the groups in my locality that made me very uncomfortable. Separate conversations were being held around the room during meetings; anonymity was being broken; articles from outside sources were being used to conduct meetings; there was interference in group affairs, etc. When I thought the problem through, I realized that many Traditions were being broken. Perhaps this was because we had several new groups in the area, or perhaps it was because the older groups and members were failing to set a good example by emphasizing the Traditions.

In my six years in Al-Anon, attending several meetings a week, serving as Group Representative and being fairly active, I had attended only one or two meetings on the Traditions and they had been boring and tedious. Even at District meetings, problems involving Traditions were never discussed.

Since then, I have chaired several meetings on the Traditions at new and older groups and have found that, with a little preparation, the meetings are interesting, informative, thought and discussion-provoking.

If you are having problems in your area, or if you want to head them off, emphasize the Traditions and make them as familiar to the members as the Steps so that the help and fellowship of Al-Anon will always be there, as it was for me.

● ● ● ● ● ● ● ● ● ●

Solving Problems Caused By Domineering Member

Our groups have been growing very fast lately. New members are attracted to a strong person, especially one who seems to champion what they want. However, this became a problem for us when the strong person was not knowledgeable about the Traditions or the Steps because she herself was too new.

Older members tried quietly to point out breaks with Tradition but were rudely shoved aside or stepped over. Feeling a deep sense of responsibility toward the group's welfare, the older members became very concerned. The strong-willed new person was elected to group office, disregarded group conscience, ran the group as she pleased, declaring "to hell with the group" when someone reminded her of the Second Tradition.

Our Group Representative, a cautious, kind, quiet long-timer handled the problem this way. She called a special business meeting and held it on the Second, Fourth and Twelfth Traditions. Many new members began to understand the necessity of group conscience. The strong-willed member took it quite personally and reacted poorly. She attended only two meetings after that.

The last one was on a spiritual theme. Again, she tried to run the meeting and ram her religious beliefs down everyone's throat. The chairman did a great job. Instead of reacting emotionally, she merely continued to say "It's great you've found such firm belief. In Al-Anon there is room for your belief and all others that may differ from it."

Unfortunately, the problem member hasn't been back. However, our group did gain from the experience. We are now focusing a great deal more on the Traditions, as hard as they are to discuss, and are trying to make them as important as the Steps because they are.

● ● ● ● ● ● ● ● ● ●

UNITY

Our common welfare should come first; personal progress for the greatest number depends upon unity.

Blow Your Troubles Away

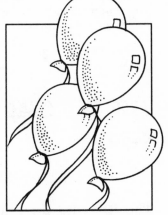

*O*ur group had been feeling some discomfort because of differences of opinion. At a recent meeting, the chairperson asked us to write down on slips of paper those things that had been disturbing us. Then she passed out brightly-colored balloons and pieces of string, inviting us to blow out those hot angry feelings, tie them up, and get rid of them.

By the time we'd laughingly completed this assignment, we were all of a mind to follow her next suggestion—discussing how our program could help us solve those difficulties.

We left the meeting feeling closer to our Higher Power and each other for the sorrow and laughter shared, and so grateful to our jewel of a chairperson.

I Need My Single Friends

*N*owhere in Al-Anon literature does it say that we learn to live with the alcoholic. Unfortunately, there are people around who, with words or attitude, give the impression that if a member separates or divorces, that person is giving up. In other words, successful program means successful marriage.

This attitude distresses me. Sometimes the only thing we can do in a difficult situation is apply Tradition One. We have

• • • • • • • • • •

to base our decisions on the good of the greatest number.

My husband and I are together, but I know I would survive and be reasonably happy if we had to separate. Al-Anon has given me that self-assurance. For too long I felt trapped. Now I'm where I am because I want to be. That's a lovely choice to have. Not everyone has that choice.

I need my single Al-Anon friends. They help me keep my perspective and are constant reminders Al-Anon is for me.

TRUSTED SERVANTS

For our group purpose there is but one authority—a loving God as He may express Himself in our group conscience. Our leaders are but trusted servants; they do not govern.

The Growing Up Tradition

The Traditions offer a wealth of valuable experience and knowledge to solve group problems. It occurred to me that I might try to apply them at home.

Tradition Two showed me how to be patient when I wasn't feeling patient; how to keep quiet when I was bursting inside to say something; how to speak when I was in no mood to; and how to listen when I felt bored.

In my group, no one has the authority to force his or her will on the rest of us. When a problem arises, we express our opinions and listen to each other. A vote on a given issue is an expression of God's will in the group conscience.

In my home, the loudest and angriest used to make all the decisions. Resentments lasted for years. Slowly, as we practiced this Tradition, we outgrew this childish behavior and became able to discuss problems calmly, express our views honestly, and cheerfully accept and live with the final decision.

● ● ● ● ● ● ● ● ● ●

When we serve in our group we are gaining self-worth. The members put their trust in those who serve. Those who lead put their trust in the members to carry on.

It took a while for this kind of trust to enter our home. For a time we competed with each other, ignored doing necessary chores, criticized each other's accomplishments. We had lists of rules.

Now there is no time or room for competition. We have thrown out the rules. A new feeling of freedom and fairness allows us to focus on ourselves. When someone accomplishes something, the whole family rejoices.

Tradition Two is my leveler. It has helped to bring happiness, serenity and balance into my life and home.

COMMON BOND

The relatives of alcoholics, when gathered together for mutual aid, may call themselves an Al-Anon Family Group, provided that, as a group they have no other affiliation. The only requirement for membership is that there be a problem of alcoholism in a relative or friend.

The Third Tradition

Several articles in *The FORUM* have touched on the question of who is eligible to belong to Al-Anon. Problems have arisen where groups have tried to keep out persons they didn't deem suitable: those who were just friends, not relatives; those who were not living with an alcoholic; those who were also alcoholic; and so on. People tend to get emotional when someone with *questionable* motives wants to belong to a group. We have had letters protesting the membership of AA members *who*, the other members imagine, *just want to spy and make*

• • • • • • • • • •

trouble, or the membership of students *who want to use us as a training ground.* There seems to be a fear that we will be exploited, that our membership will drop off, that our members won't feel comfortable about *opening up.*

If a member becomes troublesome, whether it's because of gossip, a domineering attitude, or some other factor, the First Tradition can be applied. The member can be told about the behavior the group objects to, and if necessary, the individual can be asked not to return if continuing participation would truly be detrimental to the group as a whole. But most of the time, individuals who come to meetings are there because they want help. A group's decision to ask someone not to return should not be made lightly or without every attempt to explore every other possible approach to the problem.

Tradition Three also deals with the problem of affiliation. It is easy to see the logic of it. Membership in a particular church or club should not be a prerequisite for membership in a particular Al-Anon group. And yet, we find that the line is not always so clearly drawn. We do have groups, such as institutional or industrial groups, that meet in places where it is necessary to be a patient or union member in order to have access to the building, and thus to the group. We also have groups designated for men, parents, gays, etc. How do we reconcile this?

A group may be registered provided it welcomes any Al-Anon member wishing to attend. Therefore, a woman may attend a men's group, a spouse may attend a parents' group, and so on. Members probably would not choose to do that if they had an alternative. But we all know of times when we have been in desperate need of a meeting. If the only group meeting at that time is a specialized one with whom we don't particularly identify, that should not prevent us from going there and receiving the loving support we need. Of course, we can't do anything about the rules institutions and industries have about the people who have access to their buildings. The

• • • • • • • • • • •

guideline is: if you can get there, you should be able to attend.

Very simply, the idea behind this Tradition is: let's make it as easy as possible for anyone who needs us to join us. It's not meant to be restrictive. Quite the contrary. It is meant to guarantee the right of anyone who is suffering from someone else's drinking problem to receive the help we can give them.

AUTONOMY

Each group should be autonomous, except in matters affecting another group or Al-Anon or AA as a whole.

Tradition Four

Just as in Tradition One we learn to place the welfare of the group above that of any individual member, in Tradition Four we learn that the welfare of Al-Anon or AA as a whole must come before that of any individual group. We must remember that each of us has a responsibility for safeguarding the image of Al-Anon, for seeing to it that the fellowship as a whole continues to thrive.

How a group spends its money, for instance, is a matter of group autonomy. So are the matters of having open or closed meetings, whether or not to have outside speakers, and other internal matters. What a group does becomes a problem when public opinion is involved, or when AA or Al-Anon World Service can suffer as a consequence of the group's behavior. For instance, if a group were to submit a story to a local newspaper that was very poorly written, or that contained gross misinformation about Al-Anon; or if a group were to break the Tradition of non-endorsement and come out in favor of a political candidate, or treatment center, or whatever; or if those who are in attendance at an Al-Anon function in a public place, such as a hotel or motel, behave in inappropriate ways—this can give Al-Anon a black-eye and keep away those who need the program.

• • • • • • • • • •

Neglecting to support the WSO, buying literature with group funds from publishers other than the WSO, these things hurt Al-Anon as a whole. If a group's decision will affect another group, or AA, such as a change in meeting place, or a workshop, or convention, it is important to consult those who will be affected by the decision.

Probably the best way to ensure that we keep this Tradition is to keep all the rest. By keeping ourselves strong and healthy, we help the entire fellowship.

COOPERATION

Our Al-Anon groups ought never to endorse, finance, or lend our name to any outside enterprise, lest problems of money, property and prestige divert us from our primary spiritual aim. Although a separate entity, we should always cooperate with Alcoholics Anonymous.

Discussion Of The Sixth Tradition

As Al-Anon becomes more widely recognized and respected, business enterprises look for our endorsement. Film-makers, jewelers, writers, sellers of pens, praying hands and other similar items, all would benefit if they could say they were *endorsed* by Al-Anon, or had received the Al-Anon stamp of approval.

Can you imagine the problems that would arise? Companies would want to pay us for our endorsement, and we would be besieged by business people from all sides looking for our approval. We would have to hire staff and spend days and-days reviewing each new product to make sure it was suitable. And worse, we would not have any control over what these people, whom we had endorsed, did afterward. If they turned out to be charlatans, we would get a black-eye.

● ● ● ● ● ● ● ● ● ●

And so we draw the line between cooperation and endorsement. We will help people to make films, acting as consultants in their production, if we are asked. And we never use Al-Anon funds to support anything outside of Al-Anon.

This Tradition also reminds us that there can be no such thing as an *Al-Anon retreat.* Members, as individuals, can attend retreats, and conceivably may draw heavily upon the Al-Anon program for content and inspiration. The Al-Anon name cannot properly be used to identify or publicize retreats or activities of any religious denomination. Retreats are not part of Al-Anon.

Members of groups in your area may want to plan a weekend which is an Al-Anon spiritual workshop, sponsored by Al-Anon. If by chance a retreat house is rented by Al-Anon for this purpose, care should be taken not to use the word *retreat* in announcements as it could be construed as religious affiliation.

AA, of course, is in a special category. We cannot be expected to give it financial support, but we do support it spiritually. When AA has conventions and invites Al-Anon/Alateen participation, Al-Anon is responsible for their portion of the program and assumes responsibility for Al-Anon's share of the costs involved. Similarly, while the emphasis is on us, our program and our growth, we do encourage our members to attend open AA meetings, to read the AA literature, and to invite AA speakers from time to time.

Some groups share meeting lists and Intergroup offices with AA. Again, Al-Anon shares the cost. The two fellowships are bound together in love of alcoholics and dedicated to improving the lives of victims of this disease, alcoholic and non-alcoholic. We are ever-mindful of our debt to each other.

• • • • • • • • • •

Al-Anon Retreats

Just a reminder that there can be no such thing as an Al-Anon retreat, since it is against our Traditions to affiliate with any outside enterprise. Just as we do not use our meeting time to endorse beauty aids, encyclopedias or pots and pans, we do not use it to endorse local hospitals, social workers, marriage encounters or retreats. It's hard to keep quiet about these things at meetings, especially when we've gotten so much help from them; but we must remember that the program was carefully prepared so it could appeal to anyone with an alcohol or alcohol-related problem. We don't ever want to risk turning off someone who needs us, by being so turned on to something that has nothing at all to do with Al-Anon, that we give a wrong impression

SELF SUPPORT

Every group ought to be fully self-supporting, declining outside contributions.

Discussion Of Tradition Seven

At the group level, this Tradition means we pay rent or the equivalent for our meeting place. We don't accept the *donation* of a room in a church or office building or whatever. It means we supply our own refreshments, or pay for what we use, even when we meet jointly with an AA group.

At the Information Service or Intergroup level, this Tradition means that Al-Anon pays for the telephone, office space and whatever portion of expenses is incurred by Al-Anon, if sharing space or meeting lists with AA. We don't use our employer's paper, envelopes or copying machine unless we have permission and are paying the costs.

● ● ● ● ● ● ● ● ● ●

When joining with AA for conventions, we pay Al-Anon's portion of the expenses. Likewise, we may accept that portion of the proceeds realized because of Al-Anon participation.

It's easy and tempting when funds are short to cut corners and accept outside help. In the long run, however, it can be damaging to our image, cause problems and even continue to feed our sick thinking.

Before exposure to Al-Anon, we may have developed less-than-honest attitudes which we carried with us into the program. *What they don't know won't hurt them. The world owes it to me. Everybody else does it. Take what you can while the taking's good.* These attitudes need to be re-examined in the light of the program, keeping in mind that being self-supporting is a source of dignity as well as integrity. Accepting handouts keeps us dependent and beholden, in the position of not being able to refuse doing favors, always having to defer to the giver.

Since Tradition Seven limits us in this way, sometimes it becomes difficult to meet expenses. We do need to raise money to pay our way, and often the money in the basket is not enough. What to do?

Since we are self-supporting at the group, Information Service, District and Assembly levels, fund-raising events are often held. There can be raffles, white elephant sales, auctions, pot-luck suppers, special meetings, workshops for Al-Anon and Alateen members. As individuals, members may have garage sales or other fund-raising activities, unidentified as Al-Anon events, in which they sell to the public, and they may then donate the proceeds to Al-Anon.

By having special fund-raising events, groups can pay their

● ● ● ● ● ● ● ● ● ●

running expenses (rent, refreshments, baby-sitters, literature), can pay their Group Representatives' expenses when they must travel to District and Assembly meetings, can support their Information Service, pay their share of the Delegate's and Assembly's expenses, and even do some local public information work, such as placing posters in public places or donating literature to schools, libraries, doctors' offices and churches.

Information Services and Assemblies can raise additional funds to pay for an answering service, a newsletter, public information work (radio and TV tapes), meeting lists, office space and clerical help if needed.

Being self-supporting requires effort on the part of all members in applying this Tradition of independence. The rewards to Al-Anon and Alateen in terms of integrity are worth it.

NONPROFESSIONAL

Al-Anon Twelfth-Step work should remain forever nonprofessional, but our service centers may employ special workers.

Discussion Of Tradition Eight

The concept of giving each other of our strength, experience and hope, and of giving of ourselves in service to our fellowship is an integral part of our philosophy. The entire spiritual tone of Al-Anon would be negated if there were money involved. The rewards that come to us from serving in a nonprofessional, volunteer capacity cannot be measured. They are in our hearts where they don't show. Sometimes, however, confusion arises when trying to interpret this Tradition.

We don't pay professionals, nor do we pay Al-Anon and AA members, when we invite them to speak to our groups. The Tradition is easy to interpret here.

We can see the necessity for paid workers in our Informa-

• • • • • • • • • •

tion Service Offices and the World Service Office. At the WSO, for instance, we employ Al-Anon members who are Staff Administrators responsible for service in various departments such as Public Information, Alateen and Institutions. In addition, we employ accountants, bookkeepers, record keepers, stenographers, typists, receptionists, file clerks and shipping clerks, and we retain an attorney. The tremendous amount of work that needs to be done, which is not Twelfth-Step work, would be impossible to accomplish if we had to depend on volunteers. Further, employing paid staff members ensures continuity and quality of service to the fellowship.

Sometimes, though, Al-Anon members are confused about this Tradition because some of these paid workers, as part of their every-day duties, answer the phones, write letters and deal with people in distress. Those staff members who are also members of Al-Anon give encouragement and share their experience and hope. These workers are carrying the message. They are telling outsiders about Al-Anon and Alateen, giving them information about the nearest meeting, responding to inquiries. They are prepared to give this nonprofessional Twelfth-Step help as Al-Anon members, whatever their function is as paid staff employees. They are paid only for their office work.

Many areas find that having an answering service to take distress calls is cumbersome. A troubled person finally gets the courage to call for help, and she is told someone will call her back. Many times such a person won't leave her name or number and the opportunity to help her is lost. This, more than any other factor, has prompted many localities to establish an office where there can be a volunteer to answer the phone. However, volunteers are not always available. Sometimes the paid secretary, an Al-Anon member, is the only one there to answer the phone. If it rings, should she then, because she is paid, act only in the capacity of an answering service and refer the call to another member, denying that person the immediate help and comfort she needs and for

• • • • • • • • • •

which she is reaching out? This would be terribly frustrating for the caller and for the secretary, and would negate the reason for establishing the office in the first place.

We want to preserve the concept of volunteers at every level of service: group officers, Delegates, Area Coordinators and officers, World Service Committee members and chairpersons, and Trustees. And at the same time, we want our paid employees to feel free to carry the Al-Anon message.

RESPONSIBILITY

Our groups, as such, ought never be organized; but we may create service boards or committees directly responsible to those they serve.

Discussion Of Tradition Nine

Can you imagine what meetings would be like if we had to follow parliamentary procedure, address the chairperson as *Madam Chairperson*, or had rules about people missing meetings or not getting there on time, or not putting anything in the basket? Probably no one would want to attend! Tradition Nine reminds us that at the group level, we want to preserve the feeling of informality which allows members to grow at their own pace.

Not being organized at the group level means that we have no rigid rules, no punishments, no formal procedures. However, if no one chaired the meeting, no one collected or kept track of the money, no one set up or cleaned up, there would be total chaos. And so we do elect officers and committees to assume these various responsibilities. When we look at the world-wide structure of Al-Anon, we see that the same principle holds there, too.

The important thing to remember about committees or service boards, whether they be at the group, Information Service, Assembly or World Service level, is that they are directly responsible to those they serve. This protects us against problems that might arise by appointing people to positions of authority. The idea that those who work on committees and service boards are serving those who appoint them is a key principle, one which keeps us from being filled with self-importance and driven by self-will to do what we want to, instead of what is good for the group or fellowship as a whole. It reminds us that we sometimes have to put our personal preferences aside and defer to the wishes of the majority. This Tradition, like so many others, is based on the spiritual principles of humility, service and personal freedom.

ANONYMITY

Anonymity is the spiritual foundation of all our Traditions, ever reminding us to place principles above personalities.

Humility—Antidote For Arrogance

When I felt totally inadequate, I covered up those feelings by criticizing others, looking down my nose at them, vigorously defending myself against any criticism. I reassured myself that I was lovable and desirable by constantly comparing myself favorably to others. An image of perfection was what I desperately needed to project. If someone treated me disrespectfully, I became highly insulted. It was very important for me to be recognized for my efforts. And it was very important for me to believe I didn't need anyone; they needed me.

On the other hand, I believed myself to be worthless, and was far more critical of myself than even my worst critics. I had a false notion of humility that prevented me from growing. To me, humility meant denying my strengths, never taking credit for my accomplishments, and finding fault with myself.

• • • • • • • • • •

In Al-Anon, I learned that humility is truth. It is the ability to see the good as well as the bad. It is the opposite of vanity, which is rooted in a poor self-image. For instance, the less desirable I felt, the more important it was for me to look well, to have people admire me. Now that I feel better about myself, I can accept my flaws without getting overly upset.

Once I latched onto that concept of humility as truth, I became more comfortable. It meant I could accept both compliments and criticism graciously. An honest appraisal of myself and the realization that no one should expect perfection helped me to become comfortable with the opinions of others.

But I think visualizing myself as a part of a larger whole was my most meaningful insight into humility—the realization that, in this program, it's the message that counts, not the person who is carrying it. Our Higher Power works His miracles through us and as my friend says, *even in spite of us.* Growing up means ceasing to see ourselves as the center of the universe and beginning to find our proper place in it, assuming full responsibility for the role we play.

Bill W., in his wisdom, knew that the principle of anonymity was necessary to keep the heads of AA members down to size. I think he attributed their tendency to become filled with self-importance to their alcoholism. But I have a feeling it's part of the human condition. I've certainly been aware of it in myself! All of us like to get recognition, and the less we like ourselves, the more we need it. But by making all of us anonymous servants, the program reminds us that we are but a part of a whole, and that we must measure our actions as they affect our relationship to that whole, whether it be our family, our community, Al-Anon or any other group to which we belong. To me, an important aspect of humility is knowing when and how I am needed and trying my best to fill that need; and knowing how and when I need others and allowing them to help me.

● ● ● ● ● ● ● ● ● ●

Cogent Comments

The road to happiness is always under construction.

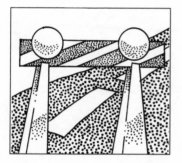

COGENT COMMENTS

Kindness is never wasted.

There is no saint without a past, no sinner without a future.

A pint of example is worth a gallon of advice.

The road to happiness is always under construction.

If I don't stay out in the sun, my tan fades; if I don't keep coming to meetings, my program fades.

An ODAT that is falling apart usually belongs to a person who isn't.

Life will always have its ups and downs, but I don't have to go up and down with it.

I am master of my unspoken words, and slave to those words that should have remained unsaid.

A man's character is like a fence: it cannot be strengthened with whitewash.

Mean what you say, but don't be mean when you say it.

Resentments come from injured pride—someone has hit us in the *I.*

Attitudes are contagious—are yours worth catching?

The depth of Al-Anon is not down, but up.

A smile happens in a flash; but the memory of it can last forever.

Winners never quit, and quitters never win.

The Twelfth-Step summed up: Let's practice what we preach.

• • • • • • • • • •

God gives only the best to those who leave the choice up to Him.

I devour my *FORUM* as soon as it arrives. The second time through, I do more chewing.

Resentment is slow-burning anger. It hurts the one who resents, not the one who is resented.

A perfectionist is a person who takes enough pains to give everyone else one.

Failure: Thinking you can't. Success: Comes in cans.

Five G's In Al-Anon

Get off his back. Get out of his way. Get onto yourself. Get to meetings. Give him to God.

Halt!

Don't be Hungry, Angry, Lonely, Tired. Do be Honest, Active, Lively, Tolerant.

The Three C's

We cannot Cause, Control or Cure alcoholism.

● ● ● ● ● ● ● ● ● ●

Index

You will find this listing of the subjects covered in our book a big help, both in planning meetings and for your personal needs.